The Crosiers
They Share with Everyone

Piet van den Bosch, O.S.C.

Translated by
Louis Van de Cruys
William McNiff, O.S.C.
Richard John, O.S.C.
Hans Van Doorn, O.S.C.
James Hentges, O.S.C.
Raymond Steffes, O.S.C.

Edited by
Michael Cotone, O.S.C.

A Michael Glazier Book
THE LITURGICAL PRESS
Collegeville, Minnesota

Religious Order Series

Volume 5

The Crosiers

A Michael Glazier Book published by The Liturgical Press

Cover design by David Manahan, O.S.B.

Cover logo courtesy of the Crosier Community

Photographs and illustrations courtesy of the Crosier Historical Institute, Bonn, Germany

1   2   3   4   5   6   7   8   9

Library of Congress Cataloging-in-Publication Data

Bosch, Piet van den.
    [Sie teilten mit jedermann. English]
    The Crosiers : they share with everyone / by Piet van den Bosch.
       p.   cm. — (Religious order series)
    "A Michael Glazier book."
    Translation of: Sie teilten mit jedermann.
    Includes bibliographical references.
    ISBN 0-8146-5836-9
    1. Crosier Fathers—History. I. Title. II. Series.
BX3493.B6313   1992
271'.19—dc20
                           92-2404
                            CIP

Contents

Foreword

In the United States the Order of the Holy Cross is more commonly known as the Crosier Order or simply the Crosiers. Although they are one of the Church's older religious communities and have lived and worked in the United States since 1910, the Crosiers have hitherto published no comprehensive history of their Order in English. This is due, in large measure, to certain events in that history.

The origins and earliest history of the Crosiers have long been an enigma. A reformation of the Order in 1410 caused the destruction of most of the documentary evidence for its history during the preceding two centuries, from the time of its foundation around 1210. Nearly all existing accounts of the Crosiers' earliest history date from after 1410, and most from a century or two later. Recent study of surviving copies of those official documents confirming the Order's existence and earliest legislation reveals that they contain significant interpolations. This in turn has raised new questions about the accuracy of later accounts of those first centuries.

The circumstances of the Order's life during the past two hundred years have created additional difficulties for its historians. The suppression of many northern European religious houses during and after the French Revolution brought the Crosiers to the brink of extinction by 1840. During this time, some of their libraries and archives were destroyed, others were confiscated and scattered across Europe. Since the Order's revival in the the middle of the nineteenth century, its members have often been too occupied with the tasks of rebuilding their religious life and serving the Church to investigate more than the essentials of their history. A concerted effort to recover significantly more of that history truly began only with the formation of the "Clairlieu Circle" of Crosier and other historians in the 1940s. Among the later members of this group was the author of this volume, the late Piet Van Den Bosch, O.S.C. (1922–1985). A native of Amsterdam, Father Van Den Bosch received his secondary education at the Crosier school in Uden before entering the Order himself in 1942. After his ordination to the priesthood in 1947, he was sent to the University of Utrecht to study history, in which he received his teaching degree in 1953. He taught history at the school in Uden for two years (1951–1953) and subsequently Church history at the Crosier major seminary in Zouterwoude (1953–1956), while also serving as the assistant moderator of a religious student union at the University of Leiden.

Between 1956 and 1974 Father Van Den Bosch was stationed in Amersfoort, where the Crosiers operated a large secondary school. During these years, he collaborated in a museum and periodical (both named *Flehite*) dedicated to the history of East Brabant, and assisted at the parish in Hamersveld. Higher studies at the University of Amsterdam, where he received his doctorate in 1968, brought him into contact with Professor J. F. Niermeyer, who encouraged his study of the life of medieval monasteries and the choice of religious observance among the Crosiers during the fifteenth century as the topic of his dissertation.

After completing his doctorate, Father Van Den Bosch devoted more of his time and energy to the study of his Order's history, frequently publishing articles in *Clairlieu,* a periodical devoted to Crosier history, and elsewhere. His goal was to better coordinate and unify Crosier historical studies and to devote himself completely to that work. Thus, in 1974, his superiors approved of and facilitated his transfer to the Crosier monastery in Bonn, Germany, where he converted a part of that building into the "Historical Institute," a center for the collection and preservation of materials and information pertinent to the Crosiers' history. This volume was written there and published in 1978 with the title *Sie Teilten mit Jedermann.*

Father Van Den Bosch's presence in Bonn and his contacts with scholars in the Netherlands, Belgium, and Germany did much to foster interest in Crosier history among those who are not members of the Order. Among his colleagues he enjoyed the reputation of a hard-working and insightful historian, whose research was methodically thorough. Being well-known in his field, he was much in demand as a speaker at gatherings of historical societies and as a contributor to scholarly publications. His sudden and untimely death in Bonn on March 29, 1985, deprived the Order of the Holy Cross of a valued confrere and historian.

In his preface to this book, Father Van Den Bosch says that his goals were to offer a provisional evaluation of the work done on Crosier history during the previous four decades and to celebrate the twenty-fifth anniversary of the Order's return to Germany in 1953. His work is, therefore, intended for both scholars and the general public.

Readers will immediately sense that the book is a celebration of the Crosiers' life and work since their foundation in the thirteenth century. Those unfamiliar with the Crosiers, or familiar only with the broad outlines of their history, will find here a respected scholar's clear and uncomplicated summary of the Order's story. At the same time, the notes and bibliography contain a wealth of references reflecting the enormous amount of research done by Crosier and other historians during recent decades and offering more scholarly readers a rich point of departure for further study.

Despite its value as an introduction to the history of the Crosiers, we must nevertheless ask ourselves whether, in Father Van Den Bosch's choice for this book of "a direction which differs from works published" previously, he has attempted more than he was able to achieve in such a short history. The reader should note that Father Van Den Bosch has used this volume to expand upon his theory, first published in 1970, that the Order of the Holy Cross began as an order of "hospitalers," that is, as a community of religious who cared for the poor, the needy, and pilgrims. Because this is a new, even somewhat revolutionary, view of Crosier origins and history, we must warn our readers that it does not enjoy unanimous acceptance among the Order's members nor its historians but does shape the way Father Van Den Bosch presents the Order's history, especially in his third and fourth chapters. Despite the novelty of his theory, Father Van Den Bosch's ideas are the fruit of his research as a professional historian and their merits will, in the end, have to be judged by his scholarly peers.

The book's value as a brief but comprehensive history of the Crosiers has led the Order's master general, Fr. Lambert Graus, O.S.C., to encourage the several efforts which have brought about its translation into and publication in English. The initial translation was made by Louis Van De Cruys, a friend of Fr. Ghislain Thevissen, O.S.C., provincial of the Belgian Crosiers, and a former teacher of English at the "Regentaat" (a school which trains teachers for the Belgian equivalent of an American middle school) in Turnhout. Fr. Richard John, O.S.C., revised the translation and prepared the appendix, with the assistance of Fr. Hans Van Doorn, O.S.C., of the Order's Indonesian Province. Extensive and thorough revision of the English text into its present form was the work of Fr. William McNiff, O.S.C., of the English department of Crosier Seminary, Onamia, Minnesota. The notes to the text were translated by Fr. James Hentges, O.S.C., with the assistance of Fr. Raymond Steffes, O.S.C. Father Hentges has also added some English-language references to the notes and bibliography. Almost all the illustrations are those found in the German original, and come from the archives of the Crosier Historical Institute in Bonn, through the kindness of Fr. Gerard Reyners, O.S.C.

The Crosiers in the United States extend their sincere thanks to all these individuals for their efforts in making Father Van Den Bosch's work available to an English-speaking readership. Additional thanks are owed to Fr. Robert Rossi, O.S.C., provincial of the Crosiers in the U.S., for his encouragement and promotion of this project, and to the staff of The Liturgical Press.

The present writer's task has been to compile the translated materials, compare them with the German original and prepare them for publication. He wishes to express his personal thanks to Frs. James Remmerswaal, O.S.C., and Adrian Van Zutphen, O.S.C., for their assistance in this, and to the Crosier Community of Onamia, Minnesota, whose congenial and fraternal atmosphere has made completion of the project significantly easier.

Michael Cotone, O.S.C.

Preface

In 1932 the Reverend Dr. Robert Haass published his dissertation on "The Crosiers in the Rhineland."[1] It was a pioneering work. Earlier scholars had studied the history of individual Crosier monasteries and had published limited material on them, but none had worked on a comprehensive history of the Crosiers who lived and worked in Germany from 1298 to 1820.

The Order is grateful to Dr. Haass for the service he has rendered it. After the secularization of monasteries in Germany at the beginning of the nineteenth century, the Order completely disappeared from that country. Although it managed to survive in the Netherlands, it did not really prosper again until the third decade of the present century and, in consequence, lacked the resources to make extensive historical studies of its past. After World War II the Crosiers in Belgium and the Netherlands were at last able to begin publishing a review devoted to their history. Called *Clairlieu* after the site of the Order's first motherhouse, it observed the thirty-fifth anniversary of its publication in 1977.[2]

Clairlieu is evidence of the intense study of Crosier history that has taken place since the pioneering work of Dr. Haass. Inevitably, later scholars have developed views on the life and the work of the

[1]R. Haass, *Die Kreuzherren in den Rheinlanden,* Rheinisches Archiv, Veröffentlichungen des Instituts für geschichtliche Landeskunde der Rheinlande an der Universität Bonn (Bonn, 1932). Dr. Haass was director of the Historical Archives of the archdiocese of Cologne from 1949 to 1968.

[2]*Clairlieu, Tijdschrift gewijd aan de geschiedenis der Kruisheren,* Kruisherenklooster, B-3581 Achel, Belgium.

Crosiers which differ from those of Dr. Haass. Inevitably, too, they have discovered that a great deal more remains to be done. The histories of many monasteries have not been studied at all and, where such study has begun, investigation continues to turn up more problems and to suggest more areas needing research.

That being the case, is it possible at this time to write even a brief history of the Order, or is the attempt an exercise in presumption? We think that we can make a provisional evaluation which will show on one hand the progress made in the study of the Order and on the other indicate the gaps which remain to be filled. Further, it seems an appropriate time to do so: in 1978 the Crosiers celebrated the twenty-fifth anniversary of their return to Germany at the invitation of Cardinal Joseph Frings.

We do not claim this to be the final word. No historical work is ever more than an incomplete attempt to find reality: there is always something more waiting to be discovered. We are aware, too, that another historian might well have approached the task differently. We have, in fact, deliberately chosen a direction which differs from works published about the Order to this date. The subtitle *They Share with Everyone* emphasizes something which has marked the Order's beginning and its work through the centuries: active ministry and the care of the needy.[3]

In his work on medieval hospices,[4] Dr. S. Reicke writes that in the Middle Ages regular clergy who attended to the needy were called

---

[3]Several seventeenth-century Crosiers wrote histories of their Order. One such, Pierre Verduc, asserted that his Order's founder was a "hospitaler," that is, a religious who cared for the sick and the poor: see P. Verduc, O.S.C., *La vie du bienheureux Théodore de Celles* (Perigeux, 1681). S. J. Helyot, *Histoires des ordres monastiques, religieux et militaires* (Paris, 1714) 2:222–241, also characterizes the Crosiers as an order of hospitalers, as does R. Hostie, *Leven en dood van de religieuse instituten* (Eammaus, 1972) 114. The latter, however, is acquainted only with Helyot. Of more importance is J. Michael Hayden, "The Crosiers in England and France," *Clairlieu* 22 (1964) 91–100, which claims that only the Crosier monasteries at Huy and in England had hospices, and that soon after the Order's foundation there was a split between these monasteries, which had hospices, and those in the Low Countries, France and the Rhineland, which did not. See also H. Van Rooijen, O.S.C., *De oorsprong van de orde der Kruisbroeders of Kruisheren. De Geschiedbronnen* (Diest, 1961). Van Rooijen repeatedly observes that, as canons regular, the first Crosiers must certainly have devoted themselves to the work of hospitality. Finally, there is also P. Van Den Bosch, O.S.C., "De orde van de Kruisheren in het verleden een hospitaalorde?," *Handelingen van het XLIe congres van de Federatie van de Kringen voor Oudheidkeit en Geschiedenis van België* (Mechelen, 1970) 173–180.

[4]S. Reicke, *Das Deutsche Spital und sein Recht im Mittelalter* (Stuttgart, 1942).

"Brethren of the Holy Cross," but does not include the Rhineland Crosiers among them. In his opinion the latter were not involved with the needy and had no hospices or other accommodations where the poor could be cared for. Although we are of a different opinion, Dr. Reicke's general thesis, that Brethren of the Holy Cross were regular clergy who ministered in hospices and homes for the poor, is absolutely correct.

In the fifteenth century there were "Brethren of the Holy Cross" all over Europe. They were so called because all of them wore some kind of cross on their habits. They did not, however, all belong to the same Order. Each Order had its own form of government and its own motherhouse. These monastic communities were founded in the late twelfth and early thirteenth centuries, and later came to be known as "Brethren of the Holy Cross."

To illustrate. The Italian Brethren of the Holy Cross, whose members wore a silver cross, were founded in 1169 and were centered in Bologna. Brethren of the Holy Cross in Spain and Portugal had their headquarters in Coimbra. Brethren of the Holy Cross who wore a red star worked in Bohemia and Silesia; others, based in Krakow, ministered in Poland. Brethren of the Holy Cross lived and worked in western Europe, too: in the Low Countries, France, Germany, England, Ireland, and elsewhere. These individuals belonged either to the Italian Brethren of the Holy Cross or to those of the Low Countries. The latter wore a red-and-white cross and were centered near the city of Huy on the Meuse River.

The name "Brethren of the Holy Cross," then, was a collective term referring to a number of Orders, just as "mendicant" is a collective term which includes the Franciscans, Dominicans, Carmelites, and Augustinians.

Like the mendicants, all Brethren of the Holy Cross had much in common. They were regular canons, that is, members of orders which celebrated the liturgy in their churches as their primary function. Choral prayer was compulsory. Unlike the Benedictines and Cistercians, however, they also devoted themselves to active ministerial work. They differed from the mendicant orders in that their monasteries owned property, which in the Middle Ages meant land.

A common and important concern of all these Brethren was ministry to and the care of the needy and distressed: the poor, the sick, and wayfaring pilgrims. Hostels or hospices could always be found in the neighborhood of their monasteries. The cross the Brethren wore on their habits symbolized their concern for those in distress.

Several other groups of clerics in Europe cared for the poor and the sick and, like the Brethren of the Holy Cross, wore a cross on their habits; others who did the same work did not wear a cross, but they too were often called "Brethren of the Cross" by their contemporaries. Even members of some lay confraternities called themselves "Brethren of the Holy Cross" because they took care of the needy.[5]

We will limit our study to the Crosiers, those Brethren of the Holy Cross who wore a red-and-white cross and who, as we noted above, had their center near the city of Huy on the Meuse River in the southern Low Countries.[6]

<hr />

[5]See Ph. I. Swoboda, *Gloriosa crucis memoria in expositione historica de ortu et progressu sacri ac antiquissimi canonici ordinis Crucigerorum cum rubeo corde, sancta Maria Demetrii de urbe, beatorum Martyrum de poenitentia sub regula divi Augustini militantes* (Prague, 1748); K. Fackler, *Das alte Memmingen* (Memmingen, 1929); M. Hörmann, *Die augustiner Chorherren in Augsburg im Mittelalter* (Bottrop, 1932); W. Hermann, *Zur Geschichte der Neisser Kreuzherren vom Orden der regulierten Chorherren und Wächter des heiligen Grabes zu Jerusalem mit dem doppelten roten Kreuz* (Breslau, 1938); P. Noordeloos, "Een bijdrage tot de geschiedenis van de Commanderie van St. Antonius van Maastricht," *Publications de la soc. hist. et arch. dans le Limbourg* 92-93 (1956-57) 153-254; W. Lorenz, *Die Kreuzherren mit dem roten Stern* (Königstein, 1964); J. Von Steynitz, *Mittelalterliche Hospitäler der Orden und Städte als Einrichtungen der sozialen Sicherung,* Sozialpolitische Schriften (Berlin, 1970); R. Vandenberghe, *Damme* (Damme, n.d.); and Sr. Hereswitha, "Orde van het Heilig-Graf," *Inleidung tot de geschiedenis van het kloosterwezen in de Nederlanden.* A: Orden onstaan in de Middeleeuwen (Brussels, 1975), 2.1ff.

[6]See also the following short histories of the Crosiers: J. Francino, O.S.C., *Geschiedenis van de Orde der Kruisheren* (Utrecht, 1948); C. Van Dal, O.S.C., *Volg mij. De Kruisheren in de Geschiedenis* (Diest, 1956); H. Van Rooijen, O.S.C., "A History of the Crosier Order. An Endeavour" (mimeographed text of a course on Crosier history delivered at the United States Crosier major seminary in Fort Wayne, Indiana, during the 1961-1962 school year); M. Vinken, O.S.C., "Croisiers," *Dictionnaire d'histoire et de géographie ecclésiastiques* 13, cols. 1042-1062, and "Croisiers," *Dictionnaire de spiritualité,* cols. 2573-2575; and H. Van De Ven, O.S.C., "Kruisheren," *Theologische Woordenboek* (Roermond-Maaseik, 1957) cols. 2819-2828.

1

The Foundation of the Order

As is the case with many Orders, the origins and the foundation of the Order of the Holy Cross which wears the red-and-white cross are hazy and uncertain. To reconstruct the story of the Order's origins, we have a number of documents which probably date from twenty to thirty years after its foundation. There are also a number of "histories" of the Order's beginnings which were written later.

These "histories" of the Order's origins were obviously written for some specific purpose. They generally agree with the stories of the origins of other Orders of the Holy Cross in Europe and probably are partially borrowed from them. Those sections of the various foundation stories which agree with each other are probably legends; the parts unique to each Order are probably based on fact.

In addition to the early documents and the later "histories," there is a third possible way to reach a better understanding of the Order.

If one searches for a river's source, one could, of course, explore the area where that source might be found. But doesn't it make more sense to follow the river upstream to its source? In the same way, cannot our knowledge of the fifteenth-century Order of the Holy Cross illumine its earlier history, and thereby give us a better understanding of the Order's origins and of the ideals of the first Crosiers? There certainly must have been a continuity: a tree is known by its fruits.

We intend to show that, in the fourteenth and fifteenth centuries, the Crosiers were asked to take over hospices in several cities and other places. Can we not assume that the Crosiers, like the mendicants, remained attached to those activities chosen by their Order at its beginnings and felt obliged to continue them? Georgius Van Bruggen, master general of Crosiers from 1452 to 1458, accepted hospices "according to the old statutes from the time of the first approval" (*iuxta antiqua primi favoris statuta*).[1] Later, in 1663, Theodorus Candidus le Blanc, O.S.C., wrote that, "[the Order of the Holy Cross] must be ranked above others because of its hospices" (*hospitii reliquis ante ferendus ope*).[2]

Most importantly, we maintain that the stories about the Crosiers' origins ought to be read from a well-defined historical starting-point: from the very beginning, the first Crosiers who wore the red-and-white cross took on themselves the additional activity of caring for the needy, or at least of the poor and of passing pilgrims.[3]

The Earliest Account of the Foundation

The earliest account of the Order's foundation, the poem *Ad Colendam Mente Pura*, is an especially attractive one. Christianus von Sittard, O.S.C., transcribed this poem sometime between 1450 and 1480.[4] The text itself, however, is much older, possibly dating from the second half of the thirteenth century. (The poem makes no mention of any dates.) Unlike other accounts of the Order's foundation, it is succinct, which argues for its authenticity.

We can summarize the first part of the poem as follows: The Order was founded by St. Helena. After finding the cross of Jesus in Jerusalem, she selected twelve men to whom she entrusted the task of protecting it. They were to wear a cross on their clothing and were given the name of "Brothers of the Holy Cross." All twelve were martyred and the Order perished.

---

[1]A. Hertzworms, O.S.C., *Religio sanctissimae Crucis* (Roermond, 1686) 82.

[2]Th. C. Le Blanc, O.S.C., *Symbolum Trinitatis* (Roermond, 1668) 124.

[3]See P. Van Den Bosch, O.S.C., "De 'Enquête' van Prof. J. le Goff," *Clairlieu* 31 (1973) 123–125.

[4]The text is found in manuscript 6 L 21, fol. 4ro–5vo, of the library of the Grand Séminaire, Liege. The Latin text with a Dutch translation was published in A. Van Asseldonk, O.S.C., "Handschriften van Kruisheren uit de XVe en XVIe eeuw over het ontstaan der orde van het H. Kruis," *Clairlieu* 3 (1944) 32–45; and in Van Rooijen, *De oorsprong*, 215–218.

Detail from the church windows of the former Crosier monastery in Cologne, now in the Church of St. Catherine at Oppenheim-am-Rhein, Germany; see note 5 to this chapter.

This first part of the story is very probably legendary. However, every legend has at its core some measure of truth, and in this case excavations conducted in the Holy Land may add something to the story. The ruins of a monastery dating from the first centuries have been found. On one of the walls there is a cross strikingly similar

Detail from the church windows of the former Crosier monastery in Cologne, now in the Church of St. Catherine at Oppenheim-am-Rhein, Germany; see note 5 to this chapter.

to the red-and-white cross worn by the Crosiers to this day.[5] Did monks with a special veneration for the cross of Christ live in that monastery?

The poet continues his story. God wanted the Order of the Holy Cross to awaken to new life and inspired five canons from "Alemannia" (Germany) to dedicate themselves to divine service in a special way. Desiring to live a common life, they requested the approval of Pope Innocent, who directed them to follow the Rule of St. Augustine. Further, in order to re-establish Helena's Guard of Honor for the Holy Cross, the Pope ordered the five canons to live under the patronage of the cross, bearing fruit by their words and deeds.

[5]The site was near the Sea of Galilee. This form of the cross is definitely an ancient one: examples occur in remains from the first Christian centuries in both the Holy Land and Rome. In the Church of St. Catherine at Oppenheim-am-Rhein there is a "Bible window" which was probably once part of the Crosier church in Cologne and seems to have been made in the same workshop as the windows in the choir of the Crosier church at Ehrenstein. One has the caption, "King Ahab has the prophets killed," and depicts the prophets as Crosiers. A reference perhaps to the martyrdom of the first twelve Brethren of the Holy Cross in Jerusalem? See E. Von Witzleben, "Kölner Bibelfenster des 15. Jahrhunderts in Schottland, England und Amerika," *Aachener Kunstblätter* 43 (1972) 227-248, and W. Jung, *Oppenheim und seine Katherinenkirche* (Königstein-im-Taunus, n.d.).

He then formally authorized the way of life he had prescribed for them with an official letter. Returning to their homeland, the five canons acquired a modest dwelling, and the Order of the Holy Cross began to flourish anew.

This second part of the story is credible, for a number of monasteries of regular canons were founded in this way.[6] The poet does not mention the date of the foundation, nor does he specify which Pope Innocent was involved. Since the Order's first official documents date from the middle of the thirteenth century, the Pope could have been either Innocent III (1198–1216) or Innocent IV (1234–1254).

The poet is also very vague about where the five canons settled: "in German lands." The earliest official documents expressly mention the realm of the prince-bishop of Liege as the site of their foundation, and that was part of the German Empire. Apparently the pope did not learn where their home was when they approached him.

What did the poet have in mind as he wrote this narrative, simply an account of how the Order of Crosiers wearing the red-and-white cross came into being? We believe that he had a second aim. He wanted to show clearly that his Order was really an Order of the Brethren of the Holy Cross, much like the other Orders of Brethren of the Holy Cross in Europe, except that it had been founded in Alemannia.

His description of the work of the first Crosiers is very terse: they were to bear fruit by their words and deeds. "Their words," obviously, refer to their preaching. But what does he mean by their "deeds"? The good example they gave to others, certainly, but nowhere does he write that these first Crosiers from Alemannia had dedicated themselves to caring for the needy.

Later Accounts of the Foundation

The Crosiers of the fifteenth and sixteenth centuries have left us additional accounts of their origins,[7] in which the legendary elements

---

[6]See E. Moreau, S.J., "L'origines des Croisiers belges," *Clairlieu* 3 (1945) 7–12, and Ch. Dereine, "Chanoines," *Dictionnaire d'histoire et de géographie ecclésiastiques* 12:353–405.

[7]The treatises *In honore summi regis* (manuscript 6 L 21, fol. 1ro–3vo, in the library of the Grand Séminaire, Liege, and manuscript 792, fol. 1ro–2ro, of the Bibliothèque Mazarin, Paris), *De inicio et privilegiis Ordinis fratrum sanctae Crucis*

From right to left, Bl. Theodore of Celles, St. Quiriacus and St. Helena as portrayed in the former Crosier church at Wickrath, Germany.

have been expanded. These accounts relate that after St. Helena found the True Cross in A.D. 233, the leadership of its twelve guardians in Jerusalem was entrusted to a man named Judas, who had shown St. Helena where the cross was hidden. Converted to Christianity, he took the name of Quiriacus, and later became the Bishop of Jerusalem. He and the Brothers of the Cross suffered martyrdom under the emperor Julian the Apostate (361–363), who renewed the persecution of Christians.

These narratives also describe more precisely the cross which the guardians in Jerusalem wore on their clothing. It was red and white, the colors symbolizing the blood and water flowing from the wounded side of Christ. This cross served two practical purposes:

(manuscript 25 D 11 in the library of the Grand Séminaire, Liege), and *Notula compendiosa de Ordinis nostri institutione* (manuscript 2763 of the Rijksarchief, Maastricht). The first two of these were published by A. Van Asseldonk in *Clairlieu* 1 (1943) 83–102, and in Van Rooijen, *De oorsprong*, 218–223. Only Van Rooijen has published the third of them, *ibid.*, 223–224.

it indicated that the Brothers of the Holy Cross were a community of regular religious, and it distinguished them from other Orders. From 1483 on the Crosier Order celebrated the feast of St. Quiriacus on May 4, the day after the feast of the Finding of the Holy Cross. The feast of St. Helena had been celebrated as a *totum duplex* since 1417 and is presumed to have been observed long before that.

It seems clear that, in describing their origins, the Crosiers not only drew on accounts of the foundation of other Orders of the Holy Cross but also believed that they had been founded by St. Helena with the assistance of St. Quiriacus. In their eyes, however, as in the eyes of other Brethren of the Holy Cross, the Order was even more ancient, antedating even St. Helena, who had only reestablished an older institution. They maintained that Pope Cletus, the third successor of St. Peter, was the Order's real founder. Touched by the plight of pilgrims to Rome who reached the city exhausted and penniless, he helped them personally and then took steps to make sure that such travelers would have proper attention and shelter in the future. To this end, he founded a monastery whose members wore a distinguishing cross, so that visitors could recognize them as the brothers of the hospice. In somewhat the same way, the guardians appointed by St. Helena had cared for the pilgrims who came to Jerusalem.[8] The accounts of the origins of the Crosiers wearing the red-and-white cross emphasize that they were true Brethren of the Holy Cross, that is, the cross they wore symbolized their assignment to assist the needy.

The accounts of the Order's origins continued to grow and collect details. The author of *Ad Colendam* had referred only to an unspecified Pope Innocent. Later versions of the story added that,

---

[8]The medieval Crosiers did not themselves invent the story of their origins nor initiate veneration of St. Quiriacus. The basis of these things were stories which they had read in old manuscripts. But which? Swoboda (see Preface, note 5) was unacquainted with the manuscripts at Liege but gives a version of the story very similar to what is found in them; his primary source was the work of Augustine Oldoini, S.J. (1612-1683). Somewhere in Europe, then, there must have existed a history of the foundation of the Crosier Order, but we have no idea of who the author was or when he wrote. As late as the seventeenth century the Crosiers at Caen (France) maintained that Pope Cletus had founded their Order, and that Pope Pius V and Pope Gregory XIV had confirmed its existence in 1568 and 1594, respectively. See A. Durand, "Le prieuré Sainte Croix de Caen," *Clairlieu* 25 (1967) 73.

St. Quiriacus. Detail of a monstrance from the former Crosier monastery in Venlo, the Netherlands.

after the Albigensian Crusade (around 1210), the five canons from Liege had gone to Rome on the advice of a papal legate, who went with them to help them present their plans to the Pope. On the feast of the Finding of the Holy Cross, they entered the Basilica of St. John Lateran just as the following verse of the sequence for the feast was being sung:

> Non sunt nova sacramenta,
> Nec recenter est inventa,
> Crucis haec religio.

(The mysteries are not new, nor is this veneration of the Cross of recent invention.)[9]

While the Pope and the cardinals were studying the canons' proposal, they discovered an ancient chronicle which said that the guardians of the Holy Cross, called the Brothers of the Holy Cross, had been killed during the sack of Jerusalem. It was the Pope's wish that the Order flourish again and expand throughout the world. The five canons, he said, should live according to the Rule of St. Augustine, and to their habits he attached the red-and-white cross. In an official letter he decreed that they should live the common life (*vita communis*), should follow local customs in food and drink, and should provide their own funds for their support.

Back in their own country, the five canons chose as their residence a place called Clarus Locus (Clairlieu), just outside the walls of the city of Huy. It was Pope Innocent's intention that this be "the place of origin" of the Order of the Holy Cross "in the lands near the sea."[10] One account even has the Pope himself explicitly assigning Clarus Locus as the "headquarters" of the new foundation.

---

[9]The tenth verse of the hymn *Laudes crucis attolamus*. See A. Van De Pasch, O.S.C., "De drie Gradualia," *Clairlieu* 7 (1949) 65–100; *Hymnarium Sanctae Agathae, bevattende de sequenties uit het Graduale van Johannes van Deventer* (Cuijk: St. Agatha, 1955); and N. Weisbein, "Le 'laudes crucis attolamus' de maître Hugues d'Orleans, dit le primas," *Revue du moyen âge latin* 3 (1947) 5–26.

[10]Van Asseldonk translates *in citra marinis partibus* as "in the lands beyond the sea." In that case, which countries would the Pope have had in mind? The Americas had not yet been discovered.

This gate to the grounds of
the Crosier monastery near
Huy, Belgium, is one of the
few remains of the Crosier
Order's ancient mother house
at Clairlieu.

Since this version of the Order's foundation dates the five canons' Roman visit to some time after the Albigensian Crusade, the Pope who received them must have been Innocent III. The foundation of the Order, then, must have taken place between 1210 and 1216, the last year of Pope Innocent's pontificate. These accounts make no attempt to establish any relationship between the crusade and the activities of the five canons.

The Crosiers would continue to reside at the site of their foundation, Clarus Locus, just outside the city of Huy, until the French Revolution. By papal decree it had been designated "source and head (*fons et caput*) of the Crosiers in the lands near the sea." In this we can see the intention of the authors of these accounts to emphasize the fact that they belonged to what was an Order of true Brethren of the Holy Cross and lived in northwestern Europe, "in the lands near the sea." Although other Orders of Brethren of the Holy Cross lived in central, eastern, or southern Europe, these Brethren had their origin and center elsewhere.

Henricus Russelius' Account of the Foundation

The accounts of the Order's foundation discussed above contain very few details. Quite different is the work of a seventeenth-century Crosier named Henricus Russelius, prior of the monastery at Suxy, in the Duchy of Luxembourg. Titled *Chronicon Cruciferorum sive Synopsis Memorabilium Sacri et Canonici Ordinis Sanctae Crucis*,[11] the work is meant to be an account of the lives of all the master generals of the Order up to the year 1618. It is a scholarly effort; Russelius states in his preface that he consulted two hundred manuscripts and books before beginning the work, and it is evident that he examined the history of the first half of the thirteenth century very carefully.

His opening chapters deal with the Cross of Christ, the finding of the Cross by St. Helena, and St. Quiriacus and his martyrdom. But then he introduces a new character: Theodore of Celles, a canon of Liege, who re-established the Order of the Holy Cross in Germany, France, England, Scotland, and the Netherlands. Russelius also speaks of "the lands near the sea."

Russelius' is the first mention of Theodore of Celles. James of Vitry and Thomas Cantimpré both knew of and wrote the biographies of numerous holy men and women who had lived in the southern Low Countries during the first half of the thirteenth century, but neither of them makes any mention of Theodore of Celles.[12] Russelius claims to have found his name in a list of the names of the priors of Clarus Locus near Huy. Theodore was, according to this list, the first prior of Clarus Locus and had died in 1236.[13]

Russelius tells us that Theodore of Celles participated in the Third Crusade (1189-1191) as a member of the retinue of Radulph of Zähringen, bishop of Liege (1167-1191), who was part of the army of Emperor Frederick Barbarossa. After the fall of Acre (July 12, 1191), Theodore visited Jerusalem, where he became acquainted with

---

[11]H. Russelius, O.S.C., *Chronicon Cruciferorum sive Synopsis Memorabilium Sacri et Canonici Ordinis Sanctae Crucis* (Cologne: H. Kraft, 1635; photo reproduction, Diest, 1964).

[12]James of Vitry (ca. 1180-1240), *Vita beatae Mariae Oigniacensis;* Thomas of Cantimpré, O.P. (ca. 1201-1270), *Miraculorum et exemplorum memorabilium sui temporis.*

[13]Van Rooijen, *De oorsprong*, 190.

the Canons Regular of the Holy Sepulcher. He developed an enthusiasm for their way of life—for their common prayer, but especially for their active ministry. The Canons of the Holy Sepulcher fed and cared for the many pilgrims who arrived in Jerusalem sick or destitute.

Russelius adds that the bishop of Liege died at Herderen on his return journey, after conferring on Theodore the office of canon of the cathedral of Liege.

This account contains some unresolved problems. We know that Bishop Radulph of Zähringen died on August 5, 1191 and that he had left the army at Acre before the city fell on July 12.[14] Moreover, Theodore could not have visited Jerusalem that summer because hostilities continued and the city was in the hands of the Muslims. However, the Canons of the Holy Sepulcher were in the crusader camp before Acre, and it is entirely possible that Theodore could have become acquainted with them there.[15] From his reading about Theodore's interest in the Canons of the Holy Sepulcher of Jerusalem, Russelius might well have mistakenly inferred that Theodore's meeting with them had occurred in Jerusalem itself.

We may also legitimately ask if Theodore actually accompanied the Bishop of Liege to the Holy Land. To answer the question, we must break it into parts, and then base our answer on probabilities.

Did Theodore accompany the bishop? It is very possible. The first Crosiers were an order of canons regular, and the accounts of their foundation always specify five canons as their founders. Canons usually came from noble families, so Theodore, who was one of the five, probably came from that social stratum, possibly the Liege-connected family of Celles who had built the proud Castle de Veves in the neighborhood of Celles-sur-Lesse in Belgium.[16] Such a back-

---

[14]See M. De Ring, "Rodolphe de Zaeringen," *Messager des sciences historiques* (1841) 83–94; and E. Schoolmeesters, "Les regesta de Raoul de Zaehringen, Prince-évêque de Liège, 1167–1191," *Bulletin de la soc. d'art et d'histoire du diocèse de Liège* 1 (1881) 129–203.

[15]See Sr. Hereswitha, "Orde van het Heilig-Graf," 74; the Canons of the Holy Sepulcher had been in Acre, not Jerusalem, since 1187.

[16]H. Van Rooijen, O.S.C., *Theodorus van Celles. Een tijds-en levensbeeld* (Cuijk, 1936). Later, in *De oorsprong,* Van Rooijen proposed that Theodore's surname was "de Seilles" and the Crosiers' first foundation was at Seilles, an island in the Meuse River. In his final discussion of the Order's origins, Van Rooijen suggested that Theodore may have been German and that his surname was von Zell or von Schenken-

ground would explain why the bishop of Liege would have known him well enough to encourage him to join the Crusade. Did Theodore actually reach the Holy Land? Again, it is very possible. From their earliest days the Crosiers have worn a cross on their habit. This may, of course, suggest their great veneration for the Cross and their enthusiasm for the spirit of the Crusades. On the other hand, their wearing of the cross as a symbol of love for others, and their early work of caring for the poor and for travelers may have been an imitation of the Canons of the Holy Sepulcher, who wore a red cross and cared for pilgrims.[17] Other orders who cared for the poor and pilgrims had done the same. Consequently, it is possible that Theodore did indeed travel to the Holy Land and had, at Acre or during his travels, become acquainted with the Canons of the Holy Sepulcher.

Russelius states that Theodore returned to his homeland (this would have been around 1191) and assumed his position as a canon of the cathedral of Liege, the office which Radulph of Zähringen had conferred on him. There he sided with the efforts begun by the papal legate, Cardinal Guido of Palestrina, to renew the common life, the *vita communis,* among the canons of the cathedral.

During this same period Theodore came into contact with Mary of Oignies (1177-1213). Neither James of Vitry nor Thomas of Cantimpré mention any connection between Theodore and Mary of Oignies, but Russelius claims that he had found reference to such a connection in a manuscript belonging to the monastery at Huy. Such a connection may indeed have existed: Mary of Oignies was in contact with many pious men and women, and Theodore may have been one of her disciples. Whatever the facts may be, Russelius lists her among the influences shaping Theodore's development and his decision to leave the cathedral chapter of Liege and start a new way of life with four other canons.

Here we must digress for a moment to take note of an ascetical movement in the southern Low Countries during the late twelfth and early thirteenth centuries. On their own initiative numbers of pious men and women decided to live in poverty and chastity. Calling them-

---

zell. See H. Van Rooijen, O.S.C., "The Church of the Holy Cross *de Claro Loco* and the True Origins of the Crosiers: A Spiritual Drama," trans. M. Cotone, O.S.C. (unpublished manuscript).

[17] Sr. Hereswitha, "Orde van het Heilig-Graf," 232.

selves "Christ's Poor," they centered their spirituality on the humanity of Christ and the celebration of the Eucharist. They sought to earn their living by manual labor, particularly by weaving, and were especially concerned for the care of the destitute, the sick, and travelers. Their dress, too, was that of the poor, a single garment of unprocessed, gray-yellow, or off-white undyed wool.

The movement attracted a considerable number of well-to-do women, who eventually formed communities and became known as "beguines." The men belonging to the movement frequently began living in community as canons regular.[18] Mary of Oignies was one of the most prominent figures in this movement. In 1207 she retired to a convent of Augustinians at Oignies-sur-Sambre (in the district of Hainaut, Belgium), where she and several companions lived in a secluded section of the convent until her death in 1213.

Russelius continues his story by telling us that Theodore went to southern France in 1209 to preach against the heresies of the Albigensians. There he formed friendships with St. Dominic and with Bishop Fulco of Toulouse, who had been driven from his city by the revolutionaries. Theodore did not remain in the south for long, returning home in either 1209 or 1210 (Russelius was unable to ascertain the precise date). But he came back with a directive from the papal legate: he was to preach the message of the Cross in his homeland and was to find other priests to help with this task.

On his homeward journey Theodore was accompanied by Bishop Fulco, who had heard of Mary of Oignies and wished to meet her. The two men traveled together to Normandy and then visited Mary. After this meeting Theodore renounced his position as a canon of Liege and took up residence near St. Theobald's chapel outside Huy in a place which the local people called Clarus Locus.

We do know that Bishop Fulco was in the southern Low Countries in 1212–1213 and that he visited Mary of Oignies.[19] Although we have no clear evidence to support Russelius' account of Theo-

[18]See A. Mens, O.F.M. Cap., *Oorsprong en betekenis van de Nederlandse Begijnen-en Bogardenbeweging* (Antwerp, 1949) and "De 'Kleine Armen van Christus' in de Brabantse-Luikse gewesten," *Ons Geestlijk Erf* 36 (1962) 282–331, 37 (1963) 129–169 and 353–401, 38 (1964) 113–144, 39 (1965) 225–271. See also B. Van Luijk, "Het Kruisherenideaal en de intensivering van de volkszielzorg in de 13e eeuw," *Het Oude Land van Loon* 16 (1961) 135–147.

[19]See Mens, "De 'Kleine Armen van Christus,' " (1962) 287.

dore's visit to southern France, a piece of later history suggests that that there may be substance to the story. By the middle of the thirteenth century, the Crosiers had established a monastery in Toulouse, the only place in France where they had done so by that date. We know that Bishop Fulco, after returning to Toulouse in 1215, showed special favor to all institutions who were helping oppose the Albigensians. If the bishop had gotten to know Theodore and the first Crosiers, it is entirely possible that he asked them to establish a community in Toulouse.

Southern France was on the heavily-traveled pilgrim routes to the Holy Land, to the holy city of Rome, and to the great shrine of Santiago de Compostella. Many monasteries cared for the pilgrims who passed through the region, and as this charitable work expanded throughout western Europe, the cross gradually became a symbol of peace and of help for those in need, rather than a symbol of war.[20] Russelius tells us that Theodore and his companions did not limit their ministry to preaching the Cross but, like the Canons of the Holy Sepulcher and "Christ's Poor," also cared for pilgrims and the poor. Even if Theodore and the first Crosiers were unacquainted with this part of France, they surely would have been pleased to know that they were welcome to settle there.

Although Russelius assigns dates extensively throughout his chronicle, he does not give the year Theodore took up residence at Clarus Locus. If, however, his sources were correct in saying that Theodore traveled with Bishop Fulco, the year must have been 1212.

In 1214, according to Russelius, Theodore and his companions applied to Cardinal Ugolino, the papal legate in Liege, for confirmation of their new foundation. The cardinal told them that the matter would have to be referred to the Pope and invited them to travel with him to Rome for the Council announced for 1215. They accepted his advice, and Pope Innocent III confirmed the Order of the Holy Cross on May 3, 1216, the feast of the Finding of the Holy Cross.

Although documentary evidence is lacking, the earliest accounts of the Order's foundation insist on the truth of this confirmation. It is possible that the Pope approved all the orders of "Brethren of

---

[20]See E. Delaruelle, "Paix de Dieu et croissade dans le chretienté du XIIe siècle," *Cahiers de Fanjeux* 4 (1969) 27-60.

B. THEODORVS DE CELLIS *magnus cultor crucifixi ob amorem ejus frequentes mentis excessus patiebatur.(chron.ord.*

Theodore of Celles at the foot of the Cross; from a seventeenth-century holy card.

the Holy Cross" at that time, including those in Italy, Spain, and Portugal, for these also claim confirmation by Pope Innocent III.

Russelius says that Theodore, who died in 1236, spent a good deal of time working in Italy because the Pope had entrusted him with the direction of the Italian Crosiers. On one occasion, he traveled to Rome with James of Vitry. This prominent Augustinian canon, the spiritual adviser of Mary of Oignies, had been named bishop of Acre and passed through Italy on his way to his diocese, but he does not mention Theodore in his account of the journey.[21]

In his book *Religio Sanctissimae Crucis* (1682), Arnold Hertzworms, O.S.C., published a number of papal documents which really pertain to the Italian Brethren of the Holy Cross. Hertzworms

---

[21]See R. Röhricht, "Briefe des Jacobus de Vitriaco," *Zeitschrift für Kirchengeschichte* 15 (1894) 97–120, and C. Huygens, *Lettres de Jacques de Vitry* (Leiden, 1960).

thought that these documents were also intended for the Crosiers wearing the red-and-white cross. Russelius may have shared this opinion, and so concluded that all the Brethren of the Holy Cross once belonged to a single Order, which the Pope placed under Theodore's guidance. However, the Italian Brethren of the Holy Cross have never claimed a connection with the Crosiers of Clarus Locus.

The Documents

According to Russelius, Theodore of Celles was succeeded in 1236 by Peter of Walcourt (*de Walcuria*), who gave the Order a more solid organization. The earliest documents[22] referring to the Crosiers date from the period of his leadership. Do they corroborate what we find in the accounts of the Order's foundation?

In 1532 John Stockem, O.S.C., wrote that the traditions of his day held that the Order was founded in 1210. According to the documents, however (including a book in which receipts and expenditures were recorded), the Order was established in 1233, when John of Eppa was bishop of Liege (1229–1238), and first received official papal confirmation in 1248.[23]

The Crosiers of the next century seem to have considered the papal bull issued by Pope Innocent IV on October 1, 1248, their charter of confirmation. When the Crosiers in Cologne were called into court in 1341 to answer a charge that they lacked papal approval, Conrad of Molendino, the procurator of the Cologne monastery, drew up a written defense which specified the confirmation of 1248, but he also maintained that the Order had been in existence for *more* than a hundred years.[24]

In granting the Crosiers their confirmation, the *privilegium commune,* Innocent IV used the same formula as in the cases of the

[22]Published in Van Rooijen, *De oorsprong,* 197–214.

[23]The text is found in manuscript 242 C, fol. 71ro, belonging to the library of the University of Liege and has been published in C. R. Hermans, *Annales Canonicorum Regularium S. Augustini Ordinis Sanctae Crucis* ('s Hertoogenbosch, 1858) 2:201, and in Van Rooijen, *De oorsprong,* 226.

[24]The text can be found in *Clairlieu* 6 (1948) 71–74; see also R. R. Post, "De oorsprong van de orde der Kruisbroeders," *Archief voor de geschiedenis van de katholieke kerk in Nederland* (1963) 243–253.

Benedictines, Augustinians, and Premonstratensians, namely, the bull *Religiosam Vitam*. This bull was usually issued only some years after a monastery's foundation. The surviving text of the bull consistently uses the word *ecclesia* (church) instead of the more usual *monasterium* (monastery) to refer to the foundation at Clarus Locus. But it is clear, from the text itself and from the other documents dating from 1248, that the Pope is addressing himself to the monastery of the Holy Cross and the Brethren of the Holy Cross (who are called "servants of the Cross," *Crucis servitores,* and "signed with the Cross," *Cruce signati*) at Clarus Locus, that is, at the Crosiers' headquarters "in the lands near the sea."[25]

Although the church at Clarus Locus was dedicated to St. Theobald, not to the Holy Cross, we would still maintain that the monastery of Clarus Locus can be identified with the Crosier monastery at Huy.

Russelius tells us that Hugh of Pierrepont, bishop of Liege from 1200 to 1229, put at the disposal of Theodore and his companions a little chapel dedicated to St. Theobald, a lifelong pilgrim who had died at Vicenza in 1066. The dedication of the chapel and its location—just outside the city, near the south gate—suggests that it had a special purpose. It was common practice in the twelfth and thirteenth centuries to build hospices just outside the walls of a city, where pilgrims might find shelter after the gates had been closed. The chapels attached to the hospices were usually dedicated to saints who had been pilgrims themselves or who had cared for pilgrims. We know, for example, that pilgrims who had returned from the great shrine of Saint James at Compostella sometimes built hostels near their own towns for other pilgrims on their way to Compostella. The chapel attached to such a hostel was usually dedicated to St. James.

Russelius adds that on one occasion Bishop Hugh visited the Crosiers living near the chapel of St. Theobald and was so impressed

---

[25]More precisely, the documents are addressed to "fratri ordinis sanctae crucis" (1240), to "priori et fratribus sanctae crucis" (April 1, 1247), to "prior et fratres ordinis sanctae crucis" (May 21, 1247), to "fratres sanctae crucis" (January 26, 1248), to "priori sanctae crucis" and "priori et fratribus monasteriis sanctae crucis" (October 1, 1248), to "prior et fratres sanctae crucis" (October 21, 1248), etc. Van Rooijen maintains that Pope Innocent IV was addressing himself to a church of the Holy Cross.

by how well they cared for the pilgrims and the sick that he promised to build them a new monastery. He died before he could carry out his promise, however, leaving the task to his successor, John of Eppa. An independent source adds weight to this. Laurent Melart, a mayor of Huy, wrote in 1641 that the Crosiers' monastery had been founded by John of Eppa, bishop of Liege, and by the knights and nobles of Huy so that the Crosiers might accommodate and care for pilgrims journeying to the Holy Land.[26]

On January 26, 1248, Henry of Guelders, bishop-elect of Liege, gave permission for the Crosiers in Huy to build a new church, for which the faithful had donated property. This clearly means that the Crosiers had been living in Huy for more than a year. The Crosiers dedicated their new church to St. Theobald. They had no choice in the matter, since the church was replacing a chapel dedicated to the saint. We do not know how long the old chapel was maintained in a useable condition; in 1828 its ruins were discovered on the grounds of the monastery, which had been suppressed at the end of the previous century.

The monastery at Huy was dedicated to the Holy Cross. Following this precedent, the Crosiers regularly dedicated their new monasteries to the Holy Cross: Namur (before 1250), Toulouse (before 1256), Caen (before 1275), Tournay (1284), Beyenburg (1298), and Cologne (1309).[27] However, existing churches and chapels taken

---

[26]See L. Melart, *Histoire de la ville et chasteau de Huy et ses antiquitez, avec une chronologie des ses comtes et évesques* (Tournai, 1641) and Hermans, *Annales,* 1:45.

[27]For which, we have the following: A document dated April 13, 1277, addressed to the "priori et conventus domus sanctae crucis huyensis"; see Hermans, *Annales,* 2:83. A document dated July 1, 1254; see Van Rooijen, *Theodorus van Celles,* 209, and Post, "De oorsprong," 245. A document from 1256, addressed to "fratri johanni, priori domus sanctae crucis"; see Van Rooijen, *Theodorus van Celles,* 229. A document from July 1290, addressed to the "domui et fratribus sanctae crucis"; see Durand, "Le prieuré Sainte Croix," 139. A document dated March 6, 1295, addressed to the "prior et fratres domus sanctae crucis iuxta Tornacum," of which a copy is preserved in the archives of *Clairlieu,* no. 405.5. A document dated April 21, 1307, addressed to the "domus sanctae crucis apud Steynhuys"; see W. Kisky and W. Knipping, *Die Regesten der Erzbischöfe von Köln im Mittelalter* (Bonn, 1901-1915) 4, no. 241. A document from 1316, "in favorem ecclesiae fratrum ordinis sanctae crucis in Colonia in honorem beatae Barbarae virg. dedicatae"; see Kisky and Knipping, *Die Regesten* 4:213, no. 958. A document dated April 12, 1311, addressed to the "domus sanctae crucis Coloniensis"; see H. V. Sauerland, *Urkunden und Regesten zur Geschichte der Rheinlande aus dem vatikanische Archiv* (Bonn, 1902-1913) 4:449, no. 1083.

over by the Crosiers were already dedicated to saints; accordingly, one can hardly claim that the prescription of 1248, that Crosier churches be dedicated to the Holy Cross, was an absolute tradition in the Order.[28]

It is not only those accounts of the Order's foundation written by Crosiers of later ages which identify the monastery of Clarus Locus with the monastery at Huy. The prior of Huy was in fact recognized as the head of the Order. In 1277, for example, Pope John XXI reconfirmed for the prior of Huy privileges previously granted. In 1286 the prior of Huy authorized the foundation of a monastery at Suxy, and in 1309 the foundation of a monastery in Cologne.[29]

Were other Crosier monasteries, dependent on Huy, included in the confirmation of 1248? The 1228 charter of the Italian Brethren of the Holy Cross lists a large number of monasteries but also a number of hospices.[30] When Pope Innocent III confirmed the Order of the Brothers of the Holy Spirit, also known as Brethren of the Holy Cross, in 1198, he extended his protection to the houses, vineyards, landed property, and gardens already belonging to the Order. The houses which he listed were hospices.[31]

Since the first Crosiers had taken on themselves the care of the needy, it is quite possible that the houses mentioned in the document of 1248 were also hospices. Of the six locations mentioned in the document, only two have been identified so far: Huy and Whaplode (in England).[32] There was a hospice in Huy and proba-

---

[28]In A. Van De Pasch, O.S.C., "De Tekst van de constituties der Kruisheren van 1248," *Hand. Kon. Comm. Gesch. Brussel* 117 (1952) 1–96, we find, in "Distinctio prima, cap. 1., de officio ecclesiae," the prescription that "item omnes ecclesias nostras in honore sanctae Crucis volumus consecrari." There is some doubt as to whether this provision actually appeared in the Constitutions of 1248. In 1787 W. Wijnants, O.S.C., compiled a list of Crosier churches and their patrons. Although his list is incomplete, it shows that few Crosiers churches were in fact dedicated to the Holy Cross (see Hermans, *Annales*, 2:199–200). The high altar of a Crosier church, however, was often so dedicated.

[29]For Huy, see Hermans *Annales*, 2:83; for Suxy, see *Analectes pour servir à l'histoire ecclésiastique de la Belgique* (Louvain, 1867) 4:332–334; for Cologne, see R. Knipping, *Niederrheinische Archivalien in der Nationalbibliotek und dem Nationalarchiv zu Paris* (Leipzig, 1904) 13, no. 81. See also Th. J. Lacomblet, *Urkundenbuch für die Geschichte des Niederrhein* (Düsseldorf, 1840–1857) 3:58, no. 78.

[30]See L. Auvray, *Les régistres de Gregoire IX* (Paris, 1896) 1:209.

[31]See Von Steynitz, *Mittelalterliche Hospitäler,* 76.

[32]See Van Rooijen, *De oorsprong,* 40–50.

bly one at Whaplode as well, since almost all the Crosier monasteries in England maintained one. If the houses listed in the document of 1248 were in fact hospices, they probably did not exist long; late in the twelfth and throughout the thirteenth century, many hospices were taken over by municipal authorities or suppressed.[33]

The origins of the Order of the Brethren of the Holy Cross who wear the red-and-white cross remain shadowed by uncertainty. Still, we believe that in the years 1211–1212, five canons under the leadership of Theodore of Celles founded a monastery at Clarus Locus in the suburbs of Huy, near a chapel dedicated to St. Theobald, and dedicated that monastery to the Holy Cross. It is possible that Innocent III authorized their way of life as early as 1216; that Innocent IV officially confirmed their Order in 1248 is certain.

They called themselves Brethren of the Holy Cross because they wished to sanctify themselves through the Cross of Christ and to preach it to others in their liturgy. They not only wanted to use their possessions to live a common life but especially to assist the needy in the name of the Cross, the symbol of love.[34]

[33]In several of the lists of the Order's monasteries compiled by Crosiers in the sixteenth and seventeenth centuries, the phrases cum reliquis or cum filiabus occasionally appear with the names of the monasteries: an indication that hospices or hostels were attached to them?

[34]See L. Honhon, O.S.C., Theodorus de Celles, Eerste generaal en stichter der Orde van het H. Kruis (Diest, 1936), and K. Elm, "Entstehung und Reform des belgisch-nederländischen Kreuzherrenordens," Zeitschrift für Kirchengeschichte 82 (1971) 292–313.

2

Structure and Administration

When the first Crosiers chose the life of canons regular, they also adopted the Rule of St. Augustine, always calling themselves "Brethren of the Holy Cross of the Order of St. Augustine" (*fratres Sanctae Crucis, ordinis Sancti Augustini*).[1]

The implications of this choice were important. In the first place, the early Crosiers chose to be an order of clerics who considered the celebration of the liturgy a primary duty. For them, the most important part of this duty was their choral prayer, which they chanted daily, one part during the night, the rest at various hours throughout the day. The high point of their day, however, was the communal celebration of the Eucharist. Second, they vowed to remain in the Order until death. Third, they shared everything, in imitation of Christ's disciples and the first Christians. All their property was held in common and was administered by one of the brethren. They wished to live like the poor, owning only the barest necessities for subsistence, and thus able to put aside something for the poor and for passing pilgrims. The Cross of Christ was the symbol of their love, and they preached it not only in word but in deed.

At the direction of Pope Innocent IV, Henry of Guelders, the bishop-elect of Liege, wrote to the Crosiers on the last day of 1248 and gave them permission to adopt the statutes, or constitutions,

---

[1]See A. Ramaekers, O.S.C., "The Crosier Order as a Canonical Order," *Lectures on Crosier Spirituality* (Fort Wayne, Ind., 1957) 32-93.

of the Dominicans as a means for regulating the details of their common life. Raymond of Penyafort, the third prior general of the Dominicans, had compiled this legislation from the constitutions of the Premonstratensians, which in turn had been based on those of the Cistercians.[2] But there were differences. In contrast to the mendicant Dominicans, the first Crosiers wanted authorization to acquire goods to be held in common, as was customary for all canons regular. They also wished to wear a distinctive habit, similar to those of the Cistercians, Premonstratensians, and Dominicans: a tunic of unprocessed off-white wool with a leather belt around the waist, a gray (later black) scapular, and a black mantle over the tunic. Most importantly, a cross was to be worn on the scapular and mantle; this cross was to have the same shape as the oldest Jerusalem crosses, with a red vertical beam and a white horizontal beam. The choice of colors may have been determined by the coat-of-arms of Theodore of Celles, but is more probably intended to recall the blood and the water which flowed from the heart of Christ.

These statutes, which were ratified sometime after 1248, contained prescriptions for, first, the liturgical ceremonies, then the matter and manner of fasting and abstinence, the admission of novices, and the taking of the three vows. They also specified a hierarchical form of administration: a prior general to govern the entire Order and a local prior for each monastery. Four councilors or "definitors," elected by the general chapter, assisted the prior general in the administration of the Order.

Until the French Revolution, the prior of the monastery at Huy also held the office of prior general. In the beginning the prior general was elected by a majority vote of those members of the Huy monastery with suffrage and the four definitors. Provisions for limiting the number of voters from Huy and including other monaster-

[2]See Van De Pasch, "De Tekst van de constituties"; A. Ramaekers, O.S.C., "De privileges der Kruisherenorde vanaf haar onstaan tot aan het concilie van Trente," *Clairlieu* 1 (1943) 9–83; Ph. Hofmeister, "Die Verfassung des holländischen Kreuzherrenordens," *Festschrift Ulrich Stutz* (Stuttgart, 1938); H. De Gruyter, O.S.C., ed., *Constitutionum Hexapla* (Zouterwoude, 1951); and W. Sangers, O.S.C., "De oudste constituties der Kruisherenorde," *Miscellanea L. van der Essen* (Brussels, 1947) 315–327, and "Predikbroeders-Kruisbroeders," *Miscellanea Gessleriana* (Antwerp, 1948) 1089–1095. See also A. Thomas, O.P., *De oudste constituties van de Dominicanen* (Louvain, 1965).

ies in the balloting for the office of the prior general were added as the Order expanded. In 1630 Rome granted the prior general the *pontificalia,* that is, the right to wear a purple mozetta, a pectoral cross and a ring, and to administer the minor orders.

The general chapter met each year at Huy. It was charged with addressing the important business of the Order and with enacting new statutes when necessary. The members of the chapter were all the priors of and one delegate from each monastery (or two, if the monastery was quite large). We have no record of any decisions made by the general chapters before 1410. In 1466 and 1498 the chapter instructed the monasteries to combine existing and new statutes, and in 1660 a revised edition of the statutes was issued.[3] After 1614 the general chapter convened only every third year.

The local prior, who held his office for life, was elected by those members of the monastery who enjoyed suffrage. Election was by a majority vote and required confirmation by the prior general. After consulting the older members of the local community, the new prior appointed a subprior, who assisted him in governing the monastery, and a procurator and a cellarer. The procurator administered the goods which the monastery acquired by donation or purchase. The cellarer was in charge of the food, drink, and clothing of the confreres.

Each monastery had its own novitiate and its own program of higher studies in philosophy and theology. Every year the monasteries were formally visited, or inspected, on behalf of the general chapter by the prior general or by one of two priors appointed for this task.

At the end of the fifteenth century, the general chapter asked the prior general to appoint vicars general, or provincials, for the monasteries in England and France. Their only tasks were to conduct visitations and handle administration in their respective regions.

In 1631 the general chapter divided that part of the Order previously known as "Germania" into the province of the Rhine and the province of the Meuse, stating that this would better safeguard the interests of the monasteries and the individual members. The monasteries situated in the pre-1559 dioceses of Liege and Utrecht became the province of the Meuse; those in the former dioceses of

[3] See A. Van De Pasch, O.S.C., *De definities der generale kapittels van de orde van het H. Kruis, 1410–1786* (Brussels, 1969).

Cologne, Münster, and Osnabrück and in the Dutch province of Friesland became the province of the Rhine. The prior general and his definitors appointed provincials from among the members of each province, and designated one monastery in each province as its common novitiate and two or three monasteries for the philosophical and theological education of its younger members. Under this arrangement, a provincial chapter was to be held each year, except in the years when the general chapter met.

By the beginning of the fifteenth century, the Order's membership had been divided into three classes: the priests, or canons, who prayed the choral office and performed pastoral ministries;[4] the lay brothers, or *conversi,* who worked in the hospices, received guests and performed household and agricultural labor; and the *donati,* who donated their fortune and themselves to a monastery (hence their name). The latter also took the three monastic vows and committed themselves to the monastery by a special pledge of obedience. Their work was much the same as that of the lay brothers.[5]

Choral prayer did not, of course, fill the priests' entire day. A good deal of time was left over for other occupations, but the statutes neither describe nor regulate the work of the Crosiers. Service to the poor, the sick, and pilgrims, which we claim was the Crosiers' secondary duty, is neither prescribed in their statutes nor mentioned in the papal or episcopal confirmations which they received. But the statutes do mention hospital attendants (*infirmarii*) and members of the Order who cared for guests (*receptores hospitum*). Further, each monastery was required to set up two dining rooms, one for the Crosiers and one in the guest quarters (*domus hospitum*). As a rule the brethren did not have access to the guest quarters, and were not to eat there.[6] All this leads us to conclude that each monastery expected guests in the ordinary course of things and was willing to accommodate them by setting up separate quarters for them.

[4]Priests served as prior, subprior, procurator, cellarer, sacristan, cantor, organist, novice master, professor, librarian, pastor, guest master, etc.

[5]Lay brothers and *donati* served as cook, baker, butcher, miller, brewer, tailor, cobbler, blacksmith, carpenter, barber, infirmarian, etc. There were also a number of brothers who worked in the fields, tended lawns and gardens, and cared for the livestock.

[6]See Van De Pasch, "De Tekst van de constituties," 53 (Capitulum V. de cibo) and 57 (Capitulum VII. de infirmis).

Unfortunately, the statutes do not specify what kind of guests were to be served, that is, they do not tell us whether these guest quarters were intended primarily for those in need.

To sum up, then. In setting up their organization and manner of life, the first Crosiers used the statutes not only of the Dominicans but also of the Premonstratensians and Cistercians. It is also worth noting that the Crosier statutes also prescribed a custom observed by the Orders from which they had drawn their legislation, namely, the *mandatum*. Every Thursday or Friday evening, the prior or, in his absence, the subprior was to wash the feet of his confreres, in imitation of Christ's action during the Last Supper.[7] Christ had said, "No slave is greater than his master; no messenger outranks the one who sent him" (John 13:16). The first Crosiers wanted to impress on those who followed them that Crosiers must always serve others, whoever they might be. In this way their actions would preach the Cross of Christ.

[7]See *ibid.,* 55-56 (Capitulum VI. de collatione), and L. Heere, O.S.C., "De oude gebruiken bij de Kruisheren," *Clairlieu* 3 (1945) 13-20.

3

The Early Expansion of the Order: 1248–1410

In this chapter we will tell how the Order of the Holy Cross grew. As we do, we will again emphasize that the Crosiers, besides celebrating the liturgy in their churches and chapels, dedicated themselves to the care of the poor, the sick, and pilgrims—a Crosier activity which has not yet received sufficient attention or emphasis.

We can show that many monasteries were founded to care for a hospice, a temporary shelter for people in need, or later assumed the management of one. Although we lack conclusive evidence for the work of other monasteries, our examination of their history has suggested that these, too, managed hospices. The particular instances will be examined below.

As was common with hospice churches, many Crosier churches were placed under the patronage of one of the so-called "hospice saints": St. James, who was honored by pilgrims to Compostella; St. Nicholas, St. Mary Magdalene, and St. Christopher, all invoked by pilgrims and travelers; St. Anthony the Abbot, St. Gertrude, St. John the Baptist, St. Lazarus, St. Catherine, St. Sebastian, St. George, and St. Roche, all invoked by the sick, especially those suffering from contagious diseases; St. Eligius and St. Cornelius, invoked by the poor; and St. Julian, the saint of hospitality. The Crosier statutes of 1248 had directed that each Crosier church was to be dedicated to the Holy Cross; in practice, however, the

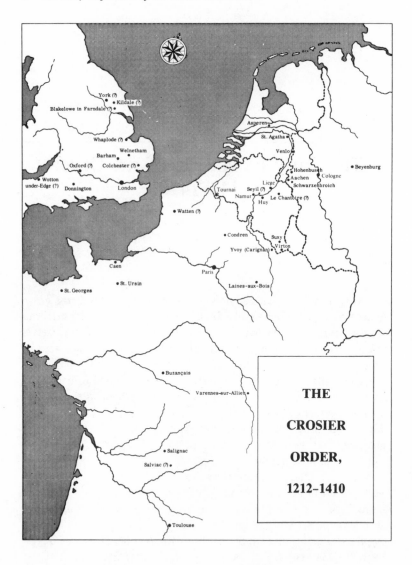

THE

CROSIER

ORDER,

1212–1410

monasteries were so dedicated more often than the churches. There must have been a significant reason for the Crosiers to retain the earlier patrons instead of rededicating the churches to the Holy Cross. It should be noted, too, that the hospice saints were widely venerated in Crosier churches, which often had altars dedicated to one or another of them.

In a number of cities, confraternities which cared for the sick, the poor, and pilgrims asked the Crosiers to settle near their churches or chapels. Tertiaries or "Beghards," who also took care of the sick, asked that the Crosiers accept their houses into the Order, too.

In many cities the Crosiers ministered to the friars and nuns who cared for hospices and helped support the chapels of the Holy Spirit, which, like the churches of the Trinity, were centers for helping the poor.

Many Crosier monasteries were located near city gates or in open country near crossroads, that is, places where pilgrims would look for a place to rest. The Crosiers also took pains to enrich their churches with the relics of saints, which would attract pilgrims.

These monasteries admitted many *donati,* which suggests that there were many individuals who had been impressed and inspired by the Crosiers' hospitality. After the sixteenth century, when pilgrimages became less common, almost every monastery had *commensales,* or paying guests.

The First Monasteries in Belgium and France

Namur[1]

The precise year of the Crosiers' first settlement in Huy cannot be determined with certainty. This complicates the correct dating of the foundations of monasteries established shortly after the mother-house.

The Crosiers settled in Namur sometime before 1250, when Henry of Guelders, the bishop-elect of Liege, granted them permission for

[1]See C. F. J. Galliot, *Histoire général ecclésiastique et civile de la ville et province de Namur* (Liege, 1788) 3; U. Berlière, O.S.B., "Les Croisiers de Namur," *Monasticon Belge* (Maredsous, 1890-1897) 1:150-152, 189-190, 462, and 490; F. Danhaive, "Le Croisiers de Namur," *Guetteur Wallon* 8 (1931) 3-36; and J. Bovesse, "Les Croisiers de Namur," *Inventaire général sommaire des archives ecclésiastiques de la province de Namur* (Brussels, 1962) 257-268.

a cemetery. Papal confirmation of the monastery was given in 1254.[2] As they had done at Huy, the Crosiers established themselves outside the north gate of Namur, near a chapel dedicated to St. Eligius. It is possible that Theodore of Celles himself had suggested the location.

An old narrative says that in 1232 the Crosiers had extended their hospitality to some passing Cistercians in a hospice near the chapel of St. Eligius.[3] Was there such a hospice near the chapel? We know that there was a well near the chapel, and that it was later enclosed within the monastery courtyard, an arrangement similar to that found at the Crosier monastery of Schwarzenbroich. This suggests that the well of St. Eligius at the north gate of Namur was one of the many "sacred wells" of medieval Europe. Pilgrims would not only wish to visit it and drink of its waters, but would also expect that the local people had provided a hospice for them nearby. In addition, the road which passed through the north gate of Namur was also part of the heavily-traveled pilgrim route to Compostella. Consequently, we should not be surprised to learn that there was a hospice dedicated to St. James near the Crosiers' monastery from which they provided liturgical services for the hospice chapel.

During the centuries the Crosiers lived at Namur in a monastery dedicated to the Holy Cross, their monastery remained a center for pilgrims who were traveling not only from Namur to Compostella but also to the famous shrine of Loreto in the Italian province of Ancona, where one could see the cottage of Mary, which had been miraculously transported there from Nazareth. It is hardly surprising, then, that Namur had a Confraternity of Our Lady of Loreto, which was based at the church of the Crosiers from its earliest years. In the early eighteenth century, when pilgrimages to Loreto began to fall off, a copy of the Cottage of Loreto was built alongside the Crosier church.[4] (The Crosier monastery located near St. Nicholas' Gate in Dinant was another center for the veneration of Our Lady of Loreto.)

The Namur community practiced the virtues of hospitality in other ways as well. They housed elderly priests in their monastery and as

[2]Hermans, *Annales,* 2:72, no. 8, and 2:77–81, no. 10.
[3]*Ibid.,* 2:74.
[4]*Ibid.,* 2:75.

late as the eighteenth century they distributed bread, meat, and beer to the poor every day and cared for ten poor families.[5] When the monastery was suppressed in 1779, the Crosiers still had not only an infirmary for their own use but a hospice next to a chapel and a guesthouse.[6] To their end, the Crosiers of Namur remained faithful to the ideals of the first Crosiers.

Toulouse

The history of the Crosier monastery at Toulouse has not yet been studied in detail. Since the oldest document dealing with the monastery dates from 1265,[7] we know that the house was established some time before that year, perhaps while Theodore of Celles was still living in Huy. We also know that the monastery, like those at Huy and Namur, was located outside the city walls and that the Crosier church was dedicated to the Holy Cross. Since southern France abounded in hospices, it seems fair to assume that the Crosiers there cared for the sick and for pilgrims.

Paris

The Crosiers came to Paris during the reign of King St. Louis (1216-1270), sometime before 1258. They first settled on the left bank of the Seine, but in 1258 Robert de Sorbonne, who needed their property for the university he was building, bought them two houses on the right bank.[8]

The biographers of King Louis tell us that he was much concerned for the poor and founded a number of hospices for them. There were already many monasteries in Paris by the middle of the thirteenth century, even though the city had not yet become a center of learning. Thus, if the king summoned the Crosiers to Paris and provided

[5]Danhaive, "Les Croisiers de Namur," 27.

[6]Bovesse, *Inventaire général,* no. 3179, "Documents relatifs à la suppression des PP. Croisiers de Namur."

[7]Van Rooijen, *Theodorus van Celles,* 229. The city archives of Toulouse contain many documents which once belonged to the Crosier monastery there. These have been microfilmed and, with similar documents from other places, compiled in a collection known as "APHOSC" (*Archivum Photographicum Ordinis Sanctae Crucis*), now kept at the Crosier monastery in Amersfoort, the Netherlands.

[8]See H. Van Rooijen, O.S.C., *Sinte Odilia, legende of historie?* (Diest, 1945). Documents from the archives of the Paris monastery have also been collected in APHOSC.

them with financial help, he must have had some well-defined and serious reason for doing so. Our opinion is, of course, that the king wanted the Crosiers to care for the poor. Their reputation for this kind of work spread: when they were asked to make new foundations in Normandy and Brittany at the end of the thirteenth century, it was primarily to care for the sick and the needy. The people who invited them there must have heard of their work in Paris.

The Monasteries in Normandy and Brittany

Caen[9]

The Crosiers arrived in Caen sometime before 1275. Here, too, they settled outside the walls of the city near one of the gates. Their

The great benefactor of the Paris Crosiers, King St. Louis IX; from a seventeenth-century engraving.

[9]See Durand, "Le prieuré Sainte Croix."

monastery was dedicated to the Holy Cross and their first church was placed under the patronage of King St. Louis, perhaps because the first members of the community had come from Paris. A document from 1359 tells us that, in that year, war destroyed both the Crosier monastery and hospice. They afterwards acquired buildings which had been occupied by the Beguines, whose chaplains they had been (as they had been in other cities). There they erected a new church and dedicated it to St. Mary Magdalene.[10]

Saint-Ursin[11]

In 1302 the Caen Crosiers founded a new monastery at Saint-Ursin, a place south of Caen and now called Ligniéres-la-Doucelle. Two hospices were placed under their care: one in Saint Ursin itself and one in Couptrain, a neighboring town. In both places, they dedicated the chapel to St. Mary Magdalene.

Trediar[12]

Forty years later the Crosiers were entrusted with the care of a hospice near Trediar, a town in Brittany. The hospice chapel was dedicated to St. George.

The Rural Monasteries

Condren

As we noted above, some Crosier monasteries were situated in the country, away from cities. Such a monastery, with a chapel dedicated to St. Eligius, was founded at Condren, a crossroads in northern France, in 1278. Travelers from Flanders, Reims, Cologne, Aix-la-Chapelle (Aachen), Liege, and Namur passed through Condren on their way to Paris, Orleans, or Tours. Such a crossroads was a natural resting place for weary travelers, but we have no substantial evidence that the Crosiers themselves conducted a hospice in Condren. (It would be well to note that St. Eligius, a seventh-

---

[10]*Ibid.,* 140-141.

[11]See A. Durand, "Le prieuré de Saint Ursin," *Clairlieu* 22 (1964) 53-90.

[12] Documents pertinent to the foundation of the monastery can be found in the Archives des Cotes-du-Nord: dossier St. Georges de Trédias, series G, 1346, 18.8.

century bishop of Noyon and Tournai, was very popular in northwestern France and was frequently the patron of hospice churches, as he was of those at Namur and Condren.)[13]

Chauny

In the fifteenth century the town of Chauny, to the south of Condren, became a new center for travelers, merchants, and pilgrims and drew off many former inhabitants of Condren. The French kings treated Chauny well, hoping that the people would give them effective support in time of war, for Chauny lay astride the road to Paris. The Crosiers settled in Chauny in 1487, near the Pissot gate, used by travelers from Cambrai and Lyons. At a later date a bastion was built in the city wall near the monastery; significantly, it was named the "Bastion-Sainte-Croix" (Holy Cross Bastion). Unfortunately no documents describing the work of the Crosiers in Chauny have survived.[14]

Reims

In 1345 Pope Clement VI informed the archbishop of Reims that he had authorized the prior of the monastery of the Holy Cross at Huy and his confreres to take over the care of St. James' Chapel in Reims and the hospice connected with it. Although the Crosiers failed to take advantage of this authorization to establish themselves in Reims, the episode shows clearly that the contemporary Crosiers were engaged in operating hospices.[15]

Salignac and Laines-aux-Bois

In the middle of the fourteenth century the Crosiers founded two more monasteries in another part of France: at Salignac, near Toulouse (1337), and at Laines-aux-Bois, in the vicinity of Troyes (1343). We cannot state with certainty why the Crosiers established these two houses.

[13]See P. Van Den Bosch, "Chauny," *Clairlieu* 30 (1972) 84–86.

[14]*Ibid.*

[15]The text of the letter, dated Decmeber 1, 1345, may be found in P. Van Isacker and U. Berlière, O.S.B., eds., *Lettres de Clément VI, 1342–1352* 1 of the *Analecta vaticana-belgica* (Brussels, 1914) 6.

Varennes-sur-Allier

At the end of the fourteenth century the Crosiers went to Varennes-sur-Allier, where they operated a hospice from 1391 until the suppression of the monastery at the end of the eighteenth century.[16]

The Monasteries in the Southern Low Countries

After founding the monastery at Namur, the Crosiers also established houses in two important cities in the southern Low Countries, Liege and Tournai, and in three other places in the region. Both Liege and Tournai were important cities during the Middle Ages. Liege was a center both of civil and ecclesiastical administration and of commerce, Tournai an ecclesiastical and commercial center. What prompted the Crosiers to settle in these two cities?

Liege

We have only a vague idea of the kind of work the Crosiers performed in this city during their first hundred years there. They had established themselves in Liege sometime before 1270, taking up residence in the rectory of the parish of St. Mary Magdalene, which was close to the city gate later named after them and near St. James' Abbey. Their own church (which may have been nothing more than a chapel built by some confraternity or other before their arrival) was dedicated to St. Matthias, who had been venerated in Liege and the diocese of Trier since 1127 and whose cult had encouraged pilgrimages to Liege. The dedication of the church to St. Matthias and the special veneration shown there to St. James and St. Mary Magdalene may simply reflect local conditions, or may indicate that the Crosiers were involved in serving the pilgrims visiting or passing through Liege.[17]

Tournai

At the invitation of Guy de Chantillon, Count of Saint-Pol, the Condren Crosiers established a house in Tournai in 1284. In a move reminiscent of the first settlement in Paris, they located their mon-

---

[16]Archives nationales, G 9, 14.

[17]See A. Van De Pasch, O.S.C., "Monastère des Croisiers à Liège," *Monasticon Belge* (Liege, 1962) 2:415-422.

astery of the Holy Cross on the right bank of the Scheldt, in a quarter whose inns were notorious—possibly to take over a hospice and improve the neighborhood's reputation. Within a few years they made their monastery church, dedicated to the Holy Trinity, a pilgrims' church. In 1287, the year that the relics of St. Odilia were transferred from Cologne to Huy, the Tournai Crosiers brought the bones of St. Languida, another of the companions of St. Ursula, to their church. Later, the Crosiers themselves built a hospice or guesthouse for travelers in Tournai. The hospice church had been a center of devotion to St. Leonard, who was also venerated in the Crosier church at Namur.[18]

Suxy

The Counts of Chiny, in the Belgian province of Luxemburg, founded two monasteries for the Crosiers. In 1286 Count Louis V turned over to them the chapel of St. Theobald at Suxy on the highway between Cologne and Rheims. Near the chapel there probably was a hospice, which the Crosiers were asked to operate.[19]

Carignan

In the same year the Crosiers also took over the chapel and a hospice at Carignan in northern France. The chapel, dedicated to St. Gertrude, was situated outside the town on the southern access road, an ancient Roman highway.[20]

Virton

The town of Virton lay between Suxy and Carignan. In 1341 the town authorities asked the Crosiers to take over the municipal hospice, located just outside the walls at the north gate. The chapel was dedicated to St. Gobergen or, perhaps later, to St. Helena.[21]

---

[18]See U. Berlière, O.S.B., "Monastère des Croisiers à Tournai," *Monasticon Belge* (Maredsous, 1890-1897) 1:460-463 and 488; and L. Heere, O.S.C., "De Kruisheren van Doornik," *Kruistriomf* (1951-1952) 2-6, 35-39, 67-70, 105-109, and 173-178.

[19]See P. Hannick, "Prieuré des Croisiers à Suxy," *Monasticon Belge* (Liege, 1975) 5:339-344. We hope to publish soon, in *Clairlieu*, a detailed review of Hannick's work and thereby substantiate the existence of the hospice.

[20]See E. Fontaine, O.S.C., "Mgr. Jacques Dubois et la fin du prieuré de Carignan," *Clairlieu* 8 (1950), 49-66.

[21]See P. Hannick, "Prieuré des Croisiers à Virton," *Monasticon Belge* (Liege, 1975) 5:345-350, and P. Roger, *Notices historiques sur Virton* (Virton, 1932) 377-397.

The Monasteries in England[22]

It is worth noting that the Crosier Order had made foundations in England during the first years of its existence, prior to 1250. It is likely that English nobility or pilgrims, traveling on the continent, became acquainted with the first Crosiers at Huy or Namur, admired their way of life and work, and encouraged them to settle in England.

Ospring, Whaplode, Colchester

The first foundations were made on the east coast of England, at Ospring in Kent, Whaplode in Lincolnshire, and Colchester in Essex. We know that the Crosiers did in fact operate a hospice at Ospring and another at Colchester, the city where St. Helena was said to have been born. At Colchester, a Confraternity of St. Helena founded a hospice which they dedicated to the Holy Cross and entrusted to the Crosiers.

Welnetham and Barham

In 1274 a monastery was founded at Welnetham in West Suffolk, not far from Colchester. The monastery or its church was dedicated to St. Thomas Becket, assassinated at Canterbury in 1170, and it is possible that the Crosiers operated a hospice for pilgrims on their way to Canterbury, the most popular place of pilgrimage in England. In 1293 the Crosiers built a monastery at Barham in Cambridgeshire, also near Colchester. They came to these towns by invitation: some noble family or a number of prominent citizens had asked them to settle there. This suggests that the work of the Crosiers in Colchester was known and respected, and that their services were in demand. To this date, however, we have no document mentioning that either of these monasteries was involved with a hospice.

[22]See E. Beck, "The Order of the Holy Cross in England," *Transactions of the Royal Historical Society,* 3rd series, 7 (1913) 191–208; J. Bulloch, "The Crutched Friars," *Records of the Scottish Church History Society* 10 (1949) 89–106; H. F. Chettle, "The Friars of the Holy Cross in England," *History. The Journal of the Historical Association* 34 (1949) 204–220; J. Michael Hayden, "The Crosiers in England and France," *Clairlieu* 22 (1964) 91–100; and D. Knowles, *The Religious Orders in England* (Cambridge, 1962) 1:204.

London

The Crosiers also settled in London. We are not sure precisely when, however. It might have been in either 1270 or 1296. The London Crosiers later called themselves a "Confraternity of Cross-Bearers"; like all medieval confraternities of this sort, they must have been involved in aiding those in need.

York and Kildale

In the fourteenth century the Crosiers tried to establish a foothold in northern England at York and Kildale in Yorkshire. Both foundations were soon closed because of the opposition of the bishop of York.

Oxford, Wotton and Donnington

An attempt was made to establish a house of studies for young Crosiers in the university city of Oxford in 1352, but it also miscarried. Two other foundations succeeded, however: at Wotton-under-Edge in Gloucestershire (1349) and at Donnington in Berkshire (1376). Twenty years after their arrival in Donnington, the founder of the Crosier monastery there built an almshouse across from the monastery. Its temporal administration was not placed in the hands

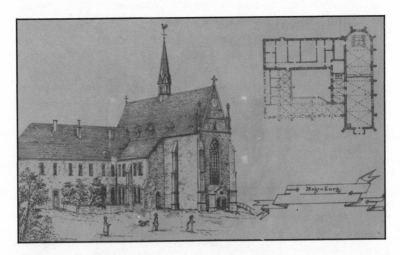

The Crosier monastery and church at Beyenburg, Germany.

of the Crosiers, however; they were to provide only for the spiritual needs of the poor.

The First Monasteries in the Rhineland

Beyenburg

The first Crosier monastery in the Rhineland was founded in 1298 at the city of Beyenburg, where the main road linking the Rhineland to Westphalia crossed the Wupper River. The city was also located on the old Hansa road from Cologne to Dortmund.

Count Adolf V (VIII) von Berg (1259-1296) invited the Crosiers to Beyenburg and gave them a chapel dedicated to St. Mary Magdalene near his mansion, called Steinhaus. His younger brother and successor, Count Wilhelm I (1296-1308), confirmed this donation. The Crosier monastery in Beyenburg was dedicated to the Holy Cross.

Considering that the nearest Crosier monastery to Beyenburg was in Liege, one wonders how the count's attention was drawn to the Order. One possibility is that he learned of the Crosiers through his brother Conrad von Berg, who was provost of the Cologne cathedral. In 1287 two Crosiers from Paris had discovered the relics of some of the companions of St. Ursula in Cologne, and it is likely that Conrad had heard of the Crosiers' work. Another possibility is that Count Adolf had himself met the Crosiers in Liege during a war which broke out between Siegfried von Westerburg, the archbishop of Cologne (1275-1297), and Duke John of Brabant. Count Adolph had allied himself to Duke John and, because the city of Liege was also among the duke's allies, it is entirely possible that Count Adolph met the Crosiers in that city in the course of the war.

The Beyenburg Crosiers were charged not only with the spiritual care of the count's domestic staff in the mansion of Steinhaus, but also with the administration of a hospice for pilgrims which we know was located near the chapel of St. Mary Magdalene, a favorite place of pilgrimage.

Large numbers of merchants and pilgrims used the bridge over the Wupper and the highways which passed through Beyenburg, making it a lively place. In 1307, shortly after their arrival, the

The former Crosier monastery at Hohenbusch, Germany.

Crosiers moved the Beyenburg monastery because the peace of the house was being disturbed by the noise from the adjoining hospice, and probably from the nearby inns. But the situation also had its compensations. The Beyenburg Crosiers were given the right to collect tolls from people crossing the city's Wupper Bridge, and held that right until the end of the eighteenth century. The reason for this arrangement was that hospice administrators (in this case, the Crosiers) were obliged to keep the road and any bridge leading to the hospice in good repair.

Duke Gerald II von Jülich-Berg (1437–1475) knew the reputation of the Crosiers as hospice administrators and asked them to take over a hospice in his own city of Düsseldorf.[23]

[23]See Haass, *Die Kreuzherren,* 42–58. At the beginning of each chapter, Haass notes the location of the surviving documents and of the monastic records which he examined. See also Th. Föhles, *Aus längst vergangenen Tagen in Beyenburg* (Beyenburg, 1930) and G. Helbeck, "Hohlwege im Beyenburger Raum: Spuren einer alten König-, Pilger-, Heer- und Hansestrasse," *Kulturgeschichtliche Bodendenkmale im Raume Wuppertal,* Beiträge zur Geschichte und Heimatkunde des Wuppertals (1976) 1:15–68.

Hohenbusch

The Crosiers also settled near a chapel on the Hohenbusch estate, not far from the town of Erkelenz. This chapel was dedicated to St. Lawrence, instead of one of the hospice saints. No record from the first centuries of this monastery's existence provides any information about its ministries, but a document of 1533 tells us that the Crosiers of Hohenbusch were "able to provide for themselves. They share with the poor and everybody."[24] But nowhere is any mention made of a hospice in the vicinity of the monastery.[25]

Cologne

In 1307 two Crosiers from Beyenburg arrived in the city of Cologne to found a monastery, which they dedicated to the Holy Cross. Their chapel, which may have already been in existence, was dedicated to St. Barbara.

The Beyenburg Crosiers may have come to Cologne to do hospice work. From the beginning, they served as chaplains to a community of Beguines who lived near the new monastery in the Streitzeugasse. (Beguines were women who did not take perpetual vows and who dedicated themselves to the care of the sick and unfortunate. Eight of them are recorded as still living in the Streitzeugasse as late as 1432.) The Crosiers also ministered to a community of Beguines in St. Anthony Street.

After 1399 the Crosiers provided the liturgy in a chapel of the Ertzelbach Hospice, where poor pilgrims found overnight lodging. In 1578 the prior was listed as an assistant of Holy Spirit Hospital, near the cathedral; he was also the visitator of the "Lungenbrüder," a community also dedicated to the care of the sick.

In 1313 four archbishops and eleven bishops granted an indulgence of forty days (something usually granted only to hospice or pil-

[24]O. Redlich, *Kirchenpolitik in Jülich-Berg am Ausgang des Mittelalters und in der Reformationzeit* (Bonn, 1907-1915) 2:724.

[25]See Haass, *Die Kreuzherren*, 59-70; J. H. Terboven, "Hohenbusch, ein ehemalige Kreuzherrenkloster," *Heimatkalendar Geilenkirchen-Heinsberg* (1965) 101-106; and G. Göller and H. Hilberath, *Musik in den Erkelenzer Landen* (Heinsberg: Kreis Heinsberg, 1972) 17-42. H. Aretz also published a number of articles about the history of the Crosier monastery at Hohenbusch in *Rheinische Post* (1976-1977). In the third (December 4, 1976), he noted that the Marian Society at Aachen (Aix-la-Chapelle) had helped underwrite the foundation of the monastery because care of the sick was one of the foremost works of the Crosiers.

An altar panel from the former Crosier church in Cologne, Germany; the Order's patron, St. Odilia, appears at the left.

grimage churches) for visits to the Crosiers' Church of St. Barbara, and in the course of the centuries, a number of Cologne burghers endowed the monastery with money to care for the poor. Although we lack any record of a Crosier hospice in Cologne, we can assume that the Brothers of the Holy Cross served the poor and the sick in that city.[26]

[26]See Haass, *Die Kreuzherren*, 71–91.

Schwarzenbroich

In 1340 the Crosiers of Liege founded a monastery at Schwarzenbroich, near the town of Düren. As in Liege, their church was dedicated to St. Matthias. Again, it is possible that Schwarzenbroich was already a center for pilgrimage and that a chapel dedicated to St. Matthias already existed when the Crosiers arrived there. We have no solid evidence that the Schwarzenbroich community formally devoted themselves to the care of the needy and pilgrims during its first century of existence, but after 1422 it did operate a hospice at Geich, on the famous old coronation, commercial, and pilgrimage route between Frankfurt and Aix-la-Chapelle (Aachen).

The monastery itself, however, was a place of refuge for many poor people and pilgrims. The poor were able to obtain food, drink, and a few nights' lodging there; pilgrims came to venerate St. Matthias and to drink from the fountain in the monastery's inner court. In 1627 Thomas Franck, O.S.C., published a small manual for pilgrims.[27]

Aix-la-Chapelle (Aachen)

In 1371 the Chapel of St. Julian near the Pont Gate of Aix-la-Chapelle was given to the Crosiers by Gertrude von Bongard; the city council turned over to them the hospice next to the chapel. This hospice provided shelter and help to the poor, to needy pilgrims, and to other travelers as well. On the occasion of the transfer, the prior general at Huy issued a circular letter in which he requested assistance for the Crosiers and promised that "The benefactors shall participate in the spiritual benefits of the Crosier monasteries and their guest houses and hospices." Monasteries and guest houses were mentioned in this circular as connected enterprises.

---

[27]See *ibid.,* 92–105. References to the Schwarzenbroich hospice may also be found in R. A. P. Van Schilfgaarde, *Het archief der Heeren en Graven van Culemborg* ('s Gravenhage, 1949) 1:409, no. 7637 (July 11, 1469) and 3:43, nos. 1942–1944 (July 8, 1469). See also H. J. Domsta, "Schwarzenbroich. Zur Ausstattung des ehemaligen Kreuzherrenklosters," *Dürener Geschichtsblätter* 54 (1970) 1417–1448; "800 Jahre Schloss und Herrschaft Merode," *Einführung der Ausstellung im Schloss von Merode bei Düren* (1974)—part of an introduction to an exhibition held in the Merode castle, near Düren—and *Geschichte der Fürsten von Merode im Mittelalter.* I. Band: Genealogie der Familie (Düren, 1974); H. Candels, *Das Prämonstratenserinnenstift Wenau* (Mönchengladbach, 1974); and P. Van Den Bosch, O.S.C., "Schwarzenbroich. Noch einmal über die Familie von Merode," *Clairlieu* 35 (1977) 114–125.

Later, in 1622, the Confraternity of St. Sebastian was founded in the Crosier church to care for those suffering from the plague.[28]

The First Monasteries in the Northern Low Countries

Asperen

In 1314, less than seven years after the Crosiers had settled in Cologne, two or three members of that community accompanied Sir John of Arkel to the County of Holland. Sir John had been so impressed by the way of life and the work of the Crosiers in Cologne that he asked some of them to return with him and settle in his city of Gorinchem. For some reason we do not know, however, the place he offered the Crosiers did not please them. Some have suggested that they might not have felt safe in a location outside the city walls, but such locations were not new to the Crosiers, who generally built their monasteries outside the gates. In any case, in 1318 they found a satisfactory site in the town of Asperen, not far from Gorinchem.

The former Crosier monastery in Aachen, Germany.

[28]See Hermans, *Annales*, 2:289-290 and 3:153; Haass, *Die Kreuzherren*, 106-115; and *Führer durch die Geschichte und die Kunstwerke der Heilig-Kreuz-Kirche in Aachen* (Aachen, 1977).

The central panel of a triptych from the Crosier monastery of St. Agatha, near Cuijk, the Netherlands. The triptych was destroyed in 1944 as a result of military action during World War II.

The foundation lasted for two and a half centuries, but disaster struck in 1567. In that year, an Asperen Crosier wrote to his confreres in Maastricht, the local lord had destroyed their residence, their church, the hospice, and the Beguine convent (suggesting that the buildings made up one complex). There is still a "Guesthouse Street" near the site of the old monastery, but we have no documents telling us about the Crosiers' work or the Asperen hospice, about their relationship to the Beguines, or about their reasons for settling in such a small town in the first place.[29]

St. Agatha

In 1367, Prior General Peter Pinchar (1364-1382), a staunch supporter of the monastery and hospice at Aix-la-Chapelle, asked John van Roermond, a Crosier of Asperen, to take over a chapel in the parish of Cuijk in the duchy of Brabant. Dedicated to St. Agatha, the chapel was located near a ferry landing on the Meuse River. It had been consecrated in 1315, and in 1342 received the so-called "collective indulgence," which was usually granted only to hospice churches: twelve bishops had granted a forty days' indulgence for works of piety connected with the chapel. The prior general's request was not carried out until 1371.

We do not know whether there was a hospice near this chapel when the Crosiers took it over, although the ruins of a small building formerly called "the Pesthouse" can still be seen not far from the chapel. The earliest document mentioning a hospice dates from 1737 and reports a fire in a hospice near the monastery.

However, we do have evidence that the monastery was devoted to the care of the sick and the poor. In 1599, the Crosiers were driven from their monastery by war and took refuge in the city of Grave. There the city authorities allowed them to operate their own grain-grinding mill, so that they could continue their long-established practice of daily distributing alms to the poor. This authorization clearly notes the character or special feature of the Order and the esteem in which the people held it. In 1647, a prior of St. Agatha stated that the monastery had never been without the presence of the poor.[30]

Venlo

In 1399 the Crosiers of St. Agatha were asked to serve a chapel in Venlo. Consecrated in 1390, the chapel was dedicated to St. Nicholas, the patron of sailors and travelers. When built, the chapel was

[29]See Hermans, *Annales,* 1:65-67, and L. Heere, O.S.C., "De Kruisheren van Asperen," *Kruistriomf* (1956) 2-7, 37-41, and 69-73.

[30]See D. Douma, "Inventaris van het archief van het Kruisherenklooster Sint Agatha, 1371-1887," *Clairlieu* 28-29 (1970-1971); L. Emond, O.S.C., "Het klooster Sint Agatha in de Lande van Cuijk," *Kruistriomf* 1-3 (1921-1924) passim; L. Heere, O.S.C., *600 Jaar Sint Agatha* (Cuijk: St. Agatha, 1971).

outside the city walls; as Venlo grew, however, the walls were extended, and the chapel and Crosier monastery found themselves inside the city. This chapel belonged to the Confraternity of St. Nicholas, an organization consisting mostly of sailors. The sailors' purpose in forming the confraternity was not merely devotional; as was customary with such medieval organizations, it was a means for providing help to the needy. It is possible that in the course of their travels the sailors had become acquainted with the Crosiers of St. Agatha and had asked members of the community to work with them in Venlo.

It is fair to assume that in Venlo, as in many other cities, the Crosiers were involved in social service, although the chroniclers of the monastery are silent about any direct responsibility they may have had for the care of the poor in Venlo. A Beguine convent and a hospice dedicated to St. George were located near the new monastery, and the Crosier community took over both buildings before 1420. They also ministered to the Hospice of St. James and gave spiritual direction to the sisters at the Chapel of the Holy Trinity.

The Black Madonna was venerated in the Crosier church in Venlo. It is reported that the number of pilgrims was always very great.[31]

A Reflection

Between 1340 and 1400 the Crosiers spread over France, England, the Low Countries, and the Rhineland. Later chroniclers, such as Russelius, mention other foundations in addition to those we have listed here. Such houses seem to have had only a brief existence, however, and we lack documentation about them.

In reviewing the expansion of the Crosier Order during its first centuries, one cannot help but be impressed by one characteristic: their hospitality toward the poor, the sick, and travelers. We know that at least thirty-five monasteries were founded, and that at least half of them operated hospices. Although we cannot substantiate

[31]See L. Heere, O.S.C., "Het Kruisherenklooster te Venlo," *Publications de la soc. hist. et arch. dans le Limbourg* 92–93 (1956–1957) 235–368, and 94–95 (1958–1959) 209–300. Around 1590 the Venlo monastery opened a kind of "retirement home" for those elderly who had no one to care for them; see J. Funken, "Das Kreuzherrenkloster in Venlo als Grundeigentümer in Leuth," *Heimatbuch des Grenzkreises Kempen-Krefeld* (1962) 177–180.

our theory in the case of each of the monasteries, we continue to hold the opinion that the constant factor in the invitations which came to the Crosiers to settle in both cities and countryside was their known hospitality. And their reputation spread further: in 1318 Pope John XXII not only confirmed their existing privileges but also authorized them to gather alms each year for their social work.[32]

Also notable during these years of expansion is the close bond between the monasteries. Every year the general chapter convened in Huy, with the prior general, the definitors, and representatives from every monastery in attendance. No new monastery could be founded nor any existing monastery enter into important obligations without the prior general's authorization. If any monastery came into difficulties with the bishop of the local diocese, it could always count on help from the prior general.

It would be erroneous, however, to think that the Crosiers were always of one heart and mind during these years. In the fourteenth century it was sometimes so difficult for the prior general to maintain unity that he twice appealed to the Pope for help, in 1340 and 1356. As discipline slackened in their monasteries, some priors refused to attend the general chapters, to obey the prior general, or to permit visitations. In these monasteries some Crosiers even acquired private incomes. When community life foundered, these monasteries ceased helping the poor and the sick. We learn from papal documents (our only source of information about these abuses) that the popes gave the prior general full authority to punish the recalcitrant Crosiers and ordered the priors of all monasteries to take part in the general chapters.[33]

We should resist the temptation to condemn the Crosiers of those times as a whole. The fourteenth century was a time in which the Church as a whole saw very few monasteries founded, but we have seen that fifteen Crosier monasteries came into existence in this century, a sign that discipline was basically still very regular and vitality strong.

The Western Schism, which lasted from 1378 to 1418, split the Church in Europe and caused a great deal of confusion. Two or three men claimed to be the legitimate pope; often there were two bishops

[32]See Ramaekers, "De privileges van der Kruisherenorde," 27-28.

[33]See Hermans, *Annales,* 2:108-117.

in one diocese and two abbots for the same abbey. Understandably, monastic discipline deteriorated rapidly, and the Crosiers were not unaffected: the monasteries in France, for example, sided with the claimant in Avignon and refused to obey the prior general, who adhered to the pope in Rome. During this period, one prior general in Huy even used bribery and influence to obtain his office.[34]

In spite of the confusion and generally bad Church leadership, a large number of Crosiers remained true to their religious life and would rouse the Order to new vigor by a reform movement in the fifteenth century. During the early years of this time of trial, they were blessed with a good leader, Prior General Peter Pinchar. Born in Caen about 1320, he chose to enter the Crosier monastery at Huy, but was called back to Caen to become prior there in 1355. He was an able theologian and renowned preacher, and during his years as prior at Caen he wrote a book called *Vestis Nuptialis* (*The Wedding Garment*), in which he impressed on his confreres the need to live as true religious and true Crosiers. This devout and learned man was elected prior general in 1364 and died in 1382.[35] Thanks largely to him, a number of Crosiers still remained truly dedicated to their religious life at the beginning of the fifteenth century, in spite of the decline in monastic discipline and in the life of the Church as a whole.

[34]The history of the monastery at Huy has been published in A. Van De Pasch, O.S.C., "Het klooster Clairlieu te Hoei en zijn prioren-generaal," *Clairlieu* 17 (1959) 65–112 and 18 (1960) 13–70, and "Monastère des Croisiers à Huy," *Monasticon Belge* (Liege, 1962) 2:405–413. See also L. Wilmotte, *Notice historique sur le couvent des Croisiers de Huy* (Huy, n.d.) and A. Joris, *Le visage de Huy* (Brussels, 1976).

[35]See C. Van Dal, O.S.C., "Rond Vestis nuptialis," *Clairlieu* 11 (1953) 3–29, and "Sint Bernardus invloed op Pierre Pinchar, O.S.C.," *Citeaux in de Nederlanden* 8 (1957) 165–180.

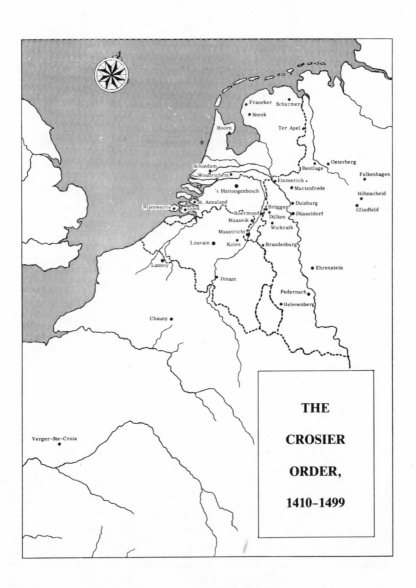

THE

CROSIER

ORDER,

1410–1499

4

The Fifteenth-Century Reformation of Crosier Religious Life

A major reform movement in the Order began in the summer of 1410.[1] Prior General John of Avins, who was not equal to the demands of his office, resigned on June 30. The next day, the definitors and the community at Huy elected Lubertus Janssen van Bommel to take his place. That same day the general chapter of the Order convened at Huy, acknowledged the new prior general, and revoked all resolutions of the former general chapters, since they deviated from canon law and the statutes of the Order. This sweeping action indicates that the members of the chapter approved of the change in leadership at Huy and accepted the reasons for it.

The movement for reform, which was demanded by the ecclesiastical authorities and probably by the secular as well, arose mainly from among the Order's superiors, who were strongly influenced by the general chapter. At this point in history, the general chapter controlled the administration of the Order more firmly than it had in earlier years. Meeting annually in Huy, it proceeded energetically to the business of reform, even overriding its original prerogatives.

[1]See P. Van Den Bosch, O.S.C., "Studien over de observantie der Kruisbroeders in de vijftiende eeuw," *Clairlieu* 26 (1968) 3–205; R. Haass, "Spätmittelalterliche Reformbestrebungen im niederrheinischen Raum und der Kreuzherrenorden," *Annalen des historischen Vereins für den Niederrhein* 144–145 (1946–47) 44–62, and "Devotio moderna in der Stadt Köln im 15. und 16. Jahrhundert," *Veröffentlichungen des Kölnischen Geschichtsvereins* 25 (1960) 134–154; and Van De Pasch, *Definities,* passim.

The general chapter strove for uniform rules and statutes, which were vitally important to its work. From the records of its annual prescriptions we learn that this governing body wanted a restoration of common life and the conscientious observance of the vow of poverty, precise observance of the laws of fast and abstinence, observance of silence in the monastery, and the wearing of the prescribed monastic habit. The list clearly reveals the faults of which many Crosiers were guilty.

The general chapter tried to achieve its aims by enlisting the active support of the priors and subpriors of the individual monasteries and by trying to prevent men who lacked the qualities of a religious vocation from entering the Order's monasteries.

The Crosier monasteries, some of which did not suffer a decline, advocated reform much earlier than other monasteries in the Low Countries and the German Empire. The renewal was unusual, too, in that it was directed from above: the superiors of the Order were quick to take the initiative, something which was most uncommon in other Orders.

The centers which initiated the Crosier reformation and served as its focal points were the monasteries at Huy, Namur, Asperen, St. Agatha, and Venlo. Later those at Liege, Cologne, and Aix-la-Chapelle (Aachen) became forces in the movement, as did the new foundations at Osterberg and Bentlage in Westphalia. Many individuals from the northern Low Countries belonged to these monasteries, and they exerted a strong influence in the movement. After 1410, those elected prior general or definitor came largely from monasteries in the Netherlands, the Rhineland, and Westphalia.

This reform movement did not go unnoticed outside the Order. As a result, the Crosiers were soon invited to establish new monasteries. After 1460 they reached a level of growth of new foundations in the Low Countries and the Rhineland which matched that of more prominent Orders.

The fifteenth-century Crosiers continued to live as canons regular, and the general chapters paid a great deal of attention to the details of celebrating the liturgy, the most distinguishing characteristic of the canonical life. Almost every general chapter of the fifteenth century issued directives for the devout celebration of the liturgical ceremonies and the observance of both the traditional and new liturgical feasts.

The general chapter had the power to transfer Crosiers from one house to another, and this probably had much to do with renewing the vigor of the Order's life, for it enabled the chapter to promote reform, help the monasteries suffering from a shortage of members, and start new foundations. However, Crosiers who were transferred never lost their connection to the monastery in which they had entered the Order. Some members were transferred quite frequently (for example, from the northern Low Countries to Westphalia or southern France) but after their travels through western Europe, they usually retired to their "home" monastery. The general chapter never failed to mention, in its annual list of deceased Crosiers, the individual's *domus nativa,* that is, the monastery in which he had entered the Order.

The fifteenth-century Crosiers continued their dedication to many forms of ministry, and it is again worth noting that they were given the care of new hospices. By the beginning of this century, however, they had entered on a new field of activity. Realizing that books are indispensable to spiritual and intellectual development, they had become very involved in copying and illuminating manuscripts and in organizing libraries. The great number of Crosier manuscripts preserved in Cologne, Düsseldorf, Liege, and Brussels bear witness to this apostolate.

The books chosen for copying show that these fifteenth-century Crosiers looked to the life and work of the old monastic orders for inspiration for their community life.[2] They also copied many of the books of the *devotio moderna.* Although the Crosier way of life was very different from that recommended by the *devotio moderna,* a strong bond of sympathy existed between the Crosiers and this movement's followers, many of whom eventually entered the Order. There

[2]See Van Den Bosch, "Studien," 153–161, and "De bibliotheken van de Kruisherenkloosters in de Nederlanden vóór 1550," *Studies over het boekenbezit en boekengebruik in de Nederlanden vóór 1660* (Brussels, 1974) 563–636; *Les manuscrits des Croisiers de Huy, Liège et Cuijk,* (Liege, 1951); A. Van Asseldonk, O.S.C., "Handschriften van Kruisheren," *Clairlieu* 14 (1956) 65–87; J.-P. Depaire, *La bibliothèque des Croisiers de Huy de Liège et de Namur* (Liege, 1969); J. Theele, "Aus der Bibliothek des Kölner Kreuzherrenklosters," *Mittelalterliche Handschriften, Festschrift für M. Degering* (Cologne, 1926) 253–263; A. van Asseldonk, O.S.C., "Keulse Kruisherenhandschriften te Wenen," *Clairlieu* 27 (1969) 47–64; K. Menne, *Deutsche und Niederländische Handschriften* 2 (Cologne, 1941); L. Heere, O.S.C., "Uit de Librije van Sint-Petersdal de Hoorn," *Clairlieu* 9 (1951) 75–79; E. Persoons, "Handschriften uit kloosters in de Nederlanden te Wenen," *Archief- en Bibliotheekwezen*

is no doubt that the movement influenced the Order; on the other hand, the members of the movement thought highly of the Crosiers because they admired them and had benefited from them. It is very likely that the *devotio moderna* profited more from Crosier advice and counsel than vice-versa.[3]

The Expansion of the Order After 1410

The campaign to reform religious observance injected new life into the Order, as the number of new monasteries founded in the Rhineland, Westphalia, and the Low Countries suggests. As had been the case before 1410, the initiative for these foundations came from noble families in the countryside and from clergymen or burghers in the towns. The Crosiers' effort to reform themselves was one of the reasons why such people now invited them to settle near their castles or in their towns and why they always set the condition that the Order's superiors should send only individuals who supported the reform.

The primary reason for such invitations, however, was that the Crosiers were wanted for some particular work or special project. When we described the expansion of the Order in the thirteenth and fourteenth centuries, we felt it necessary to emphasize that the early Crosiers had decided that the care of the poor, the sick, and pilgrims would be one of their chief activities. We know that a number of the new foundations were also involved in this work, and we can offer clues pointing in the same direction for others. There are, however, some monasteries about which we know nothing, either because they enjoyed only a brief existence or because their records have been lost.

in België 38 (1967) 59–107; O. Gatzweiler, *Die liturgischen Handschriften des Aachener Münsterstifts* (Münster, 1926); E. Gotenberg, "Die Handschriften der Kölner Kreuzbrüder" (unpublished manuscript, 1957); W. Wetzel, "Paläographische Beobachtungen an datierten Handschriften des Kölner Kruezbrüderskloster" (unpublished manuscript, 1968); J. Vennenbusch, *Die theologischen Handschriften des Stadtarchivs Köln*, Teil I: Die Folio-Handschriften der Gymnasiabibliothek (Mitteilungen aus dem Stadtarchiv von Köln), (Cologne and Vienna, 1976); and J. Kirschbaum, *Liturgische Handschriften aus dem Kölner Fraterhaus St. Michael am Weidenbach und ihre Stellung in der Kölner Buchmalerei des 16. Jahrhunderts* (Bonn, 1972).

[3]See Van Den Bosch, "Studien," 153–161, and "Thomas van Kempen en de Kruisheren," *Archief voor de geschiedenis van de katholieke Kerk in Nederland* 13 (1971) 277–307.

The Monasteries with Hospices

Bentlage

In 1437 Heinrich von Mörs, bishop of Münster, transferred the chapel of St. Gertrude at Bentlage, near Rheine, to the Crosiers. A document dating from 1495 tells us that a hospice and an almshouse stood near the monastery gate. Since the chapel there was dedicated to St. Gertrude, it can be assumed that both buildings antedated the arrival of the Crosiers. According to the chronicle of the Bentlage Crosiers, the monastery consistently attracted large numbers of the poor, and in 1573 the community complained that their revenues were insufficient to provide all their dependents with food and drink. A legend about the sanctity and hospitality of one of the monastery's guest masters, Lubertus, began to circulate shortly after his death in 1481.[4]

A gable from the former Crosier monastery in Bentlage, Germany.

[4]See H. U. Weiss, *Die Kreuzherren in Westfalen* (Diest, 1963) 117–165, 230–286; H. Büld, *Rheine an den Ems, Chroniken und Augenzeugenberichte, 1440–1950* (Rheine, 1977) 11–56; and Hertzworms, *Religio sanctissimae Crucis*, 100–101.

Düsseldorf

In 1483 Duke Gerhard von Jülich-Berg invited the Crosiers to the city of Düsseldorf, where he had his own residence. He turned over to them the Chapel of Our Lady at one of the city gates. Attached to the chapel was a hospice which cared for the sick and the poor and provided accommodations for pilgrims, many of whom visited the chapel to venerate the Mother of God. The hospice was transferred to the Flingerstrasse in 1450, but the Crosiers remained closely associated with it, and in 1549 they were also given the administration of the poorhouses in the Liefergasse.[5]

Brandenburg

In 1477 Sir Gilles von Brandenburg and his wife Margarete von Sombreff asked the Crosiers to take up residence in their castle and turn it into a monastery, promising to build them not only a new church, but a guest house beside the church. Many people came to the church as pilgrims to venerate relics of St. Anthony the Abbot and St. Odilia.[6]

Helenenberg and Bitburg

The reputation of the Crosiers as competent administrators of hospices eventually reached the ears of Johann von Baden, the archbishop of Trier, and of his chancellor, Ludolf von Enschringen. In 1485 the chancellor invited them to assume direction of a shelter for the sick, the poor, and pilgrims on the ancient Roman road between Trier and Bitburg. The building was very old, but the chancellor had it renovated. Reflecting their devotion to St. Helena, the Crosiers named the new establishment "Helenenberg" (Mount Helena); they also encouraged devotion to St. Valentine, who was invoked in cases of epilepsy and for the prevention of diseases of cattle. Helenenberg became a popular pilgrimage site, especially for people from

---

[5]See Haass, *Die Kreuzherren*, 116–132; F. L. Greb, "Zwei Gnadenbilder in der St. Lambertuskirche zu Düsseldorf," *Die Gottesmutter, Marienbild in Rheinland und Westfalen*, ed. L. Küppers (Recklinghausen, 1974) 127–151; and P. Van Den Bosch, O.S.C., "Düsseldorf. Ein Rückblick auf eine Ausstellung," *Clairlieu* 35 (1977) 95–106.

[6]See Haass, *Die Kreuzherren*, 166–169; A. Buchet, *Le prieuré des Croisiers de Brandenbourg à Raeren, 1477-1784* (Verviers, 1948); H. Reiners, *Die Kunstdenkmäler van Eupen-Malmedy* (Düsseldorf, n.d.); and P. Van Den Bosch, O.S.C., "Brandenburg," *Clairlieu* 35 (1977) 93–95.

The former Crosier church in Düsseldorf, Germany.

A seventeenth-century
engraving of the saintly
Lubertus (d. 1481).

A chasuble from the Crosier
monastery at Helenenberg,
Germany.

The former Crosier monastery at Brandenburg, near Aachen, Germany.

The former Crosier monastery at Helenenberg, Germany.

Luxemburg. The Crosiers operated a tavern in connection with this hospice, as they did near their monasteries at Brandenburg and Marienfrede.

In 1633 the town of Bitburg turned the hospice of St. John the Evangelist over to the Helenenberg Crosiers with the understanding that they would assume the chaplaincy, take care of the patients, and distribute alms to the poor. The Crosiers also pledged themselves to organize a school there.[7]

A fifteenth-century chasuble from the Crosier monastery at Ehrenstein, Germany.

[7]See Haass, *Die Kreuzherren,* 193–201; *Die Kunstdenkmäler der Rheinprovinz* (Düsseldorf: Landkreis Trier, 1936), 145–156; and E. Lichter, "Strassenbau am Ausgang des Kurstaates Trier," *Neues Trierisches Jahrbuch* (special edition, 1964) and *Welschbillig und Umgebung* (Trier, 1977).

Ehrenstein

In 1487 Bertram von Nesselrode, the lord of Ehrenstein near Neustadt-on-the-Wied, established a monastery for the Crosiers next to his castle. He intended that the monastery should operate a hospice, but was unable to found one until twelve years later, in 1499. This hospice of which the Crosiers formally assumed direction in 1501, was located near the former von Nesselrode family residence at Oetgenbach.[8]

Later they may also have directed a hospice in Waldbreitbach in the Wiedbach valley. An old crucifix, to which many miracles were attributed, was found there in 1667 and attracted pilgrims and other people from the Helenenberg area. In 1694, the pastor of Waldbreitbach, Bartholomew Friderici, O.S.C., built a chapel there and dedicated it to the Holy Cross.[9]

Pedernach and Rhens

In 1497 Archbishop Johann von Baden of Trier gave the Crosiers the Church of St. James and the neighboring monastery at Pedernach, northwest of Boppard, and in 1500 attached the hospice at Rhens to the new monastery. Although the charter of the Pedernach foundation does not state that the Crosiers were to operate a hospice in Pedernach itself, one may assume that this was part of the plan. The church was dedicated to St. James, a pilgrim's saint, and the new settlement's founder was an archbishop already acquainted with the Crosiers precisely because of their good work in hospices.[10]

Duisburg

In 1498 the Crosiers acquired the monastery of Sankt-Peterstal in Oderich on the outskirts of Duisburg. The building had formerly belonged to the Tertiaries, an organization which looked after the sick. Upon transfer of the property, four of the Tertiaries joined the Crosiers and were thus able to continue living in the same monastery. The Crosiers continued the work of the Tertiaries; the town's old chronicles frequently mention the care that the Crosiers gave the

[8]See Haass, *Die Kreuzherren,* 184–192.

[9]See E. Lichter, "200 Jahre neue Wallfahrtskirche Helenenberg bei Welschbillig," *Neues Trierisches Jahrbuch* (1966) 90–101.

[10]See Haass, *Die Kreuzherren,* 215–217.

sick and the poor, for which they received a steady flow of funds. Later, Catholic students of the University of Duisburg lived in the monastery.[11]

Falkenhagen

In 1432 Count Bernd the Elder von Lippe and his brother Simon, later the bishop of Paderborn, gave the Crosiers a monastery at Falkenhagen, near Höxter. The Crosiers built a hospice opposite the monastery. They were expelled from the monastery in 1596, however, and the Jesuits who took over the buildings turned the hospice into a church.[12]

The former Crosier monastery at Falkenhagen, Germany.

[11]See *ibid.*, 218–224, and G. Von Roden, *Geschichte der Stadt Duisburg.* Bd. I: Das alte Duisburg von den Anfängen bis 1905 (Duisburg, 1970) 250–251.

[12]See Weiss, *Die Kreuzherren in Westfalen*, 91–116; E. Kittel, "Das Kreuzherrenkloster Falkenhagen," *Dona Westfalica Georg Schrüber zum 80. Geburtstag* (Münster, 1963) 137–166; W. Huenecke, *Das Kloster Lilienthal und die Gemeinde Falkenhagen* (Detmold, 1897); and P. Van Den Bosch, O.S.C., *Das Kloster Lilienthal zu Falkenhagen* (Falkenhagen, 1978).

Höhnscheid

In 1468 Count Walram von Waldeck asked the Crosiers to move into the monastery of Höhnscheid. Associated with the monastery were a guest house and a boarding house in which food was distributed. The monastery was suppressed in 1527.[13]

Sneek, Franeker, and Ter Apel

The Crosiers also acquired hospices in the northern Low Countries. The first was the Hospice of St. Anthony in Sneek, entrusted to them in 1464; again, the Tertiaries who had been working there joined the Crosiers.[14]

In 1468 the Crosiers settled in another Frisian town, Franeker, where they were again given a hospice to manage. Today we have no way of knowing whether or not the Crosiers lived up to the expectations of the burghers of Franeker. In 1581 the town authori-

The former Crosier monastery at Höhnscheid, Germany.

[13]See Weiss, *Die Kreuzherren in Westfalen,* 166-176, 287-290.

[14]See L. J. Van Apeldoorn, *De Kerkelijke goederen in Friesland* (Leeuwarden, 1915) 2:247 and 445.

ties complained that the members of the Order had indeed organized the guest house, but not for the sake of the poor. This complaint, however, was lodged after the Crosiers had already been driven from the town by the Calvinists. The Franeker Crosiers of that time may have been admitting paying guests, as many Crosier monasteries did later in their history.[15]

In Ter Apel, where they arrived in 1466, the Crosiers managed a guest house in which they lodged pilgrims and travelers free of charge. The monastery and church burned down in 1472, but the church was rebuilt within a year and ready to be reconsecrated in honor of the Holy Cross. As was the case in other Crosier churches, the Ter Apel Crosiers enthusiastically fostered devotion to St. Anthony the Abbot, one of the most popular hospice saints. It is possible that the Ter Apel guest house antedated the coming of the Crosiers and may itself have been dedicated to St. Anthony.[16]

The Other Monasteries

We know that after 1410 many Crosier monasteries were involved in the operation of hospices; they had assumed full responsibility for fourteen of them and directed a total of about thirty. In the case of other Crosier monasteries, however, the relationship of religious house and hospice is not so clear; we simply have no way of knowing whether the operation of such a shelter was a part of either the original or a later plan for the monastery. But considering the emphasis which the Order as a whole put upon such work, it is reasonable to assume that many of the new houses did care for the poor, and that some of them may well have operated hospices at one or another point in their histories. All we have to work with, however, are the fragmentary histories of the individual houses.

Roermond

In 1422 the Confraternity of St. Cornelius at Roermond in the Netherlands asked the Crosiers to take care of their chapel, which was located near the Nieler Gate. Since the confraternity was founded

[15] See *ibid.*, 1:125 and 2:259; and A. Telting, "Het Kruisbroedersklooster te Franeker," *Vrije Vries* 9 (1862) 104–112.

[16] See A. F. Schuitema Meyer, *Het klooster Ter Apel* (Groningen, 1966).

to help the sick, it is probable that it operated a hospice in conjunction with the chapel, but neither the foundational charter or any subsequent monastery document mentions such a hospice. There was a dormitory for laymen in the monastery, however, and in medieval times such a dormitory was often used to care for the sick. In 1445 the Roermond Crosiers, like their confreres in other cities, were appointed chaplains to the Celle Sisters, a group of medieval nurses.

Several citizens of Roermond gave the Crosiers parcels of land on condition that the revenue be distributed among the poor, indicating that they wished to support the Crosiers' work and provide for its future.

Paying guests lived in the monastery from the sixteenth century until its suppression at the end of the eighteenth century. The existence of such quarters suggests that, in earlier centuries, non-paying guests who knocked at the monastery gate could also find shelter there.

In 1782 the prior of Roermond wrote the prior of St. Agatha that he hoped that his monastery would not be suppressed by Emperor Joseph II because "We take care of the sick and assist the dying." Was he referring to the Roermond Crosiers, or to the Order as a whole?[17]

Maaseik

In 1476 the Confraternity ot St. James in Maaseik (Belgium) asked the Crosiers to come to that city and assume care of the confraternity chapel. In almost every city in which it was established, the confraternity operated a hospice next to its chapel; as in Roermond, however, neither the foundational charter or any later documents of the Maaseik community say anything about a hospice associated with the Chapel of St. James, although the charter does mention the accommodation of paying guests in the monastery.

It is possible that by 1476 the number of pilgrims traveling to Compostella had begun to fall off, and the confraternity wished to put their facilities at the disposal not only of pilgrims going to Spain

[17]See J. T. J. Jamar, *Inventaris van het archief van het klooster der Kruisheren te Roermond* (Maastricht, 1973); and L. Heere, O.S.C., "Het Roermondse Kruisherenklooster," *Publications de la soc. hist. et arch. dans le Limbourg* 76 (1941) 5–49, and "Het Obituarium der Kruisheren van Roermond," *Publications de la soc. hist. et arch. dans le Limbourg* 90–91 (1954–1955) 51–125.

but of the local people in need as well. Who better to handle this task than the Crosiers? The floor plan of the Maaseik monastery is still extant. The guest room was spacious: sixty-five feet long and twenty-three feet wide, with a small adjoining room which could be heated and was also intended for guests. We can assume that these rooms in fact formed a hospice in the medieval sense of the word: a shelter for travelers, pilgrims, and the poor.[18]

Maastricht

The foundational charter of the Maastricht monastery tells us that in 1438 the Crosiers settled near the Brussels Gate in order to provide overnight accommodations for members of the Order passing through the city. The charter also states that from the very beginning the Maastricht Crosiers intended to take paying guests into the monastery. This is hardly surprising; the community needed the income to support a house whose chief purpose was to provide shelter for traveling Crosiers.

As time passed, however, they expanded their activities into familiar fields and began to minister to the Celle Brothers, who, like the Celle Sisters, cared for the sick. In 1529 seven Crosiers who had been caring for victims of the plague died; their deaths seem to have interested the local prior, Johannes Proenen (1528-1543), in medical science and caused him to purchase books on the subject. After 1530 the Maastricht Crosiers also cared for the local Holy Spirit chapel, as did the Crosiers in Venlo who managed the center for social assistance in that city.[19]

---

[18]See *De Kruisheren te Maaseik, 1476-1797, 1855-1955* (Diest, 1955); L. Heere, O.S.C., "Inventaris van het archief van het Kruisherenklooster te Maaseik" (unpublished manuscript, 1961), and "Prieuré des Crosiers à Maaseik," *Monasticon Belge* (Liege, 1976) 4:243-251; J. Coenen, "De Pastoors van Heppeneert," *Miscellanea Gessleriana* (Antwerp, 1948) 290-298; A. Van Asseldonk, O.S.C., "Marginalia bij 'De pastoors van Heppeneert,' " *Clairlieu* 8 (1950) 67-80; and R. Janssen, "De Maaseiker Historiografie," *Maaslandse Sprokkelingen* n.s. 4 (1978).

[19]See H. P. A. Van Hasselt, O.S.C., "Geschiedenis van het klooster der Kruisheren te Maastricht," *Publications de la soc. hist. et arch. dans le Limbourg* 39 (1903) 1-137; and L. Heere, O.S.C., "Zielzorg in de kapel van de Grote Heilige Geest te Maastricht," *Maasgouw* 81 (1962) cols. 175-180.

Other Monasteries in the Low Countries

Several other monasteries were founded in this region in the fifteenth century, but we have only scanty information about their work. In 1428 the Crosiers settled in the town of Goes, where they founded a Crosier Confraternity, which is said to have acquired a good deal of money. This confraternity cared for the needy and operated an orphanage and an almshouse, to the great satisfaction of the civil authorities. When Pope Pius V (1566–1572) wanted to transfer the Crosiers' property to the new bishop of Middelburg, the authorities joined the Crosiers in appealing the decision, begging the Pope not to suppress the monastery because of the valuable service which it performed for Goes and the whole region. The Crosiers, the people of Goes said, offered their choral prayer in praise of God and for the welfare of the citizens of their town, and they always extended a wholehearted welcome to religious and to secular clerics who wished to use their guest quarters.[20]

A Crosier monastery was founded in 1443 near the Kethel Gate of the city of Schiedam. At that time the Crosiers were allowed to celebrate Mass in a hospice, but we do not know whether there was a special connection between them and the hospice. We do know, however, that paying guests lived in the monastery from its very beginning. The Schiedam Crosiers organized an annual fund-raising tour in the various parishes and churches of the southern part of the County of Holland.[21]

The northern part of the county was canvassed by Crosiers from the monastery at Hoorn. In 1461 the Tertiaries there joined the Crosiers, as they had at Sneek and Duisburg; it is possible that these Tertiaries, like those in Sneek and Duisburg, may have also operated a hospital, but we have no way of knowing. We do know that the Hoorn community admitted paying guests. In 1490 Beguines

[20]See Hermans, *Annales,* 3:70–74; F. C. M. Römer, "De kloosters in Goes," *Zeeuwse Volksalmanak* (1845) 6–19; and R. A. S. Piccardt, *Bijzonderheden uit de geschiedenis der stad Goes* (Goes, 1865) 16–17, 146, 162–163.

[21]See A. J. Van De Ven, "Het Kruisbroedersconvent te Schiedam," *Bijdragen voor de geschiedenis van het bisdom Haarlem* 43 (1925) 368–422; and J. F. Sandburg, "Archivalia van het klooster der Kruisbroeders te Schiedam 1443–1554" (unpublished and undated manuscript belonging to the Algem. Rijksarchief of 's Gravenhage).

settled across from the monastery, which was located outside the city walls.[22]

In 1468 a number of Beghards (laymen living semi-monastic lives) joined the Order in the city of 's Hertoogenbosch. These Beghards made their living by working as weavers, and often looked after the sick and the poor as well. Those who chose not to join the Order caused trouble, so the Crosiers changed their residence to a building later known as "The Crosier Shelter," which was near St. Catherine's Chapel in the neighborhood of a watergate in the southern part of the city. We do not know whether this chapel was a hospice chapel, but the report of an episcopal visitation made in 1515 says that the Crosiers' prior was the only person able to give the bishop information about difficulties in two of the city's hospices. The prior was probably involved in the administration of both shelters, which would indicate that the 's Hertoogenbosch Crosiers, too, were active in one of the Order's traditional ministries. (It should be added here that many pilgrims came to the Crosier church to venerate a miraculous cross.)[23]

In 1474 the Crosiers remodeled the tollhouse near the Hof Tower of Woudrichem as a monastery and, in 1481 and 1499 respectively, settled in two places in Zeeland, Nijenwerve and Sint-Annaland. None of these three foundations have left us many documents which shed light on their work or history.[24]

In 1489 the Crosiers took over a parish in Scharmer, near Groningen. All we know of this establishment is that membership in the monastery increased steadily.[25]

---

[22]See C. J. Gonnet and R. D. Baart De La Faille, *Inventaris van het archief der stad Hoorn* (Haarlem, 1918); S. Drost, O.S.C., "Geschiedkundig overzicht van het Kruisherenklooster te Hoorn," *Geschiedk. Bladen* 2 (1906) 177–190; and L. Heere, O.S.C., "Het Sint-Petersdal of het Kruisbroederklooster te Hoorn," *Cruciferana* n.s. 22 (1964).

[23]See J. Francino, O.S.C., "Onder Maria's bescherming," *In Cruce Vita. De orde der Kruisheren in Nederland* (Rotterdam, 1936) 63–98; P. Gerlach, O.F.M. Cap., "Tijd en milieu van Jeroen Bosch," *Brabants Heem* 12 (1969) 117; and A. M. Frenken, "De latere kerkvisitaties," *Bossche Bijdragen* 27 (1963–1964) 29.

[24]For Woudrichem, see L. Heere, O.S.C., "De Kruisbroeders van Woudrichem," *Clairlieu* 8 (1950) 34–49; for Nijenwerve, see *Monasticon Batavum* 2:137; and for Sint-Annaland, see *Monasticon Batavum* 2:10.

[25]See P. Van Den Bosch, O.S.C., "De Priorij Sint Helena te Scharmer," *Clairlieu* 33 (1975) 3–30.

In addition to the monastery at Maaseik, three other Crosier houses were founded in the southern Low Countries in the fifteenth century: at Kolen-Kerniel in 1438, at Lannoy in 1474, and at Dinant in 1490.

In 1432 Maria van Kolen, a Beguine, put a number of estates at Borgloon at the disposal of the Crosiers, with the idea of helping them establish a monastery there. The Crosiers accepted her offer and soon built a church and monastery. There was some sort of trouble between them and the pastor of Borgloon, however, and the Crosiers soon left the town. Maria van Kolen sold the buildings to the Tertiaries at Zepperen and then made a second attempt to establish a Crosier monastery, this time at Kolen-Kerniel, near Borgloon. This effort succeeded, and the Crosiers settled there in 1438. Why Maria van Kolen was so eager to establish a Crosier monastery is not clear, but since she sold the Borgloon monastery to the Tertiaries after the Crosiers left, it seems likely that, as a Beguine, she wanted regular clerics to settle in Borgloon to care for the needy.

St. Odilia, the patron of the Crosiers, was the object of special devotion at Kolen-Kerniel. In the eighteenth century Martin Aubée, a well-known artist from Liège, was commissioned to paint scenes from the life of St. Odilia for the panels above the choir stalls in the church. To this day there is a Well of St. Odilia in the narthex. It is safe to assume that in times past many pilgrims prayed there, as they prayed at St. Eligius' Well in the inner court of the Crosier monastery at Namur and at St. Matthias' Well in the inner court of the Schwarzenbroich monastery. No document mentions a hospice or guest house at Kolen-Kerniel.

St. Mary Magdalene was also venerated at Kolen-Kerniel, as she was in other Crosier monasteries. A tombstone there dating from 1512 bears an image of the crucifixion, with St. Mary Magdalene and a Crosier kneeling at the foot of the cross. There is a similar representation on the reredos of the Crosier church in Maaseik.[26]

In 1474 a Crosier monastery was founded near the Tournai Gate of the city of Lannoy, at the invitation of John, the lord of the district. We do not know why he asked the Crosiers to come to his city.

---

[26]See A. Van Asseldonk, O.S.C., "Franciscus Vaes van Tongeren," *Clairlieu* 15–16 (1957–1958); A. F. Marcus, *Klooster Marienlof Kolen-Kerniel* (Beeringen, 1972); and L. Heere, O.S.C., "Prieuré de Kolen à Kerniel," *Monasticon Belge* (Liège, 1976) 6:253–259.

In the seventeenth century the Lannoy Crosiers founded two confraternities in their church, one in honor of St. Roche, the other in honor of St. Anthony the Abbot, both hospice saints.[27] In 1490, again for reasons we do not know, the burghers of Dinant asked the Crosiers to settle in their city, near St. Martin's Gate. In time the Dinant Crosiers built a chapel in honor of Our Lady of Loreto, as their confreres had done in Namur. Travelers to Dinant, who may well have stopped at the chapel to pray to the Mother of God, reported that it was a very beautiful building.[28]

The year 1490 also saw the establishment of another Crosier monastery in France, this time at Verger.

The fifteenth-century Crosiers established five monasteries in the Rhineland.

In 1444, in the parish of Dingden, they took over a monastery of the Canons Regular of Schoonhoven (the Netherlands), whose attempt to develop an active monastery there had failed. The Crosiers called their new monastery, which stood on the road to Xanten, Marienfrede. Their church was dedicated to St. Anthony the Abbot, a popular hospice saint. We have no concrete evidence of there being a hospice connected with the monastery, but we do know that people gave the Dingden Crosiers property whose revenue was intended for the poor. In 1469 a couple gave money to the monastery for bread to be baked on specified days; two-fifths of the bread was to go to the monastery and three-fifths was to be distributed to the poor at the monastery gate. The Dingden Crosiers also operated an alehouse opposite the church, a ten-minute walk from the monastery; it can be assumed that they gave shelter to travelers there.[29]

We know that the monastery at Brüggen, founded in 1479, also received a number of endowments for the poor—one, for example, in 1541 to care for thirty-three people. Although no hospice was mentioned at the time of its foundation, the monastery church was dedi-

[27]See J. Van Den Bosch, O.S.C., "Le couvent des Croisiers de Lannoy, 1474–1792," *Clairlieu* 13 (1955) 3–43.

[28]See Hermans, *Annales*, 2:262–263; U. Berlière, O.S.B., "Monastère des Croisiers à Dinant," *Monasticon Belge* (Maredsous, 1890–1897) 1:148–150, 188–189; Bovesse, "Les Croisiers de Namur," 256; C. Close, *Dinant. Notes d'histoire et de folklore* (Brussels, n.d.) 20–32; and J. Gaier-Lhoest, *L'évolution topographique de la ville Dinant au moyen âge* (Brussels, 1964) 43–44.

[29]See Haass, *Die Kreuzherren*, 132–147.

cated to the hospice saints Nicholas and Catherine, and in 1751 the Brüggen Crosiers stated that they had given food and drink to the poor every day. The monastery also cared for the parish of Born.[30]

In that same year of 1479, a Crosier monastery was founded at Dülken, near Brüggen. This monastery was given the task of establishing a school, in which two or three Crosiers were to teach. The community was itself very poor, and we have no indication that it worked with the needy.[31]

In 1478 the Crosiers went to Emmerich, and in 1480 to Wickrath. Some time previous the Asperen Crosiers had established a kind of outpost in Emmerich where they stayed during their fund-raising rounds in that city and the surrounding countryside. Much later the monastery became a haven for priests expelled from the Netherlands. Unfortunately, we do not know whether the Emmerich Crosiers carried on the Order's familiar work of caring for the poor.[32]

The former Crosier church and monastery in Brüggen, Germany.

[30]See *ibid.,* 170–180, and B. Röttgen, *Brüggen und Born im Schwalmtal* (Kempen, 1934).

[31]See Haass, *Die Kreuzherren,* 148–154, and F. Bohr, *Aus dem alten Dülken* (Viersen, 1976).

[32]See Haass, *Die Kreuzherren,* 155–165, and *Emmerich. 1200 Jahre Gymnasium* (Emmerich, 1952).

When the Crosiers took over care of the parish in Wickrath, they also assumed responsibility for the direction and the funds of the Confraternity of Our Lady and Sts. Fabian and Sebastian, a well-endowed organization dedicated to helping the poor. In 1491 the Crosiers, as they did so often, committed themselves to providing food for the poor of Wickrath.[33]

In addition to these three monasteries in Westphalia, the Crosiers set up two more foundations in this part of the German Empire: at Osterberg near Osnabrück in 1432, and at Glindfeld near Medebach in 1499. In the foundational charter of the Osterberg house, the Crosiers are called "hospitable people," but there is no mention of any hospice or program for helping the poor.[34]

The former Crosier monastery at Glindfeld, Germany.

[33]See Haass, *Die Kreuzherren,* 202–214; H. P. A. Van Hasselt, O.S.C., "Geschiedenis van het klooster der Kruisheren te Wickrath," *Geschiedk. Bladen* 2 (1906) 17–37; J. Husman and Th. Trippel, *Geschichte der ehemaligen Herrlichkeit bzw. Reichsgrafschaft und der Pfarre Wickrath* (Giesenkirchen, 1911); and R. Brandts, *Inventar des Archivs der Pfarrkirche St. Antonius in Wickrath,* Landschaftsverband Rheinland, Inventare nichtstaatlicher Archive (Düsseldorf, 1957).

[34]See Weiss, *Die Kreuzherren in Westfalen,* 69–90, 210–218.

The Glindfeld monastery, like that at Höhnscheid, stood on the old Heidenstrasse, an ancient commercial and military road. Of this monastery it has been written:

> An average of fifteen poor people were cared for every day, and received provisions for the next day. Twice a week there was a large distribution of alms, to which the poor of the whole neighborhood flocked in great numbers and at which they were given a quarter of a large loaf of bread. It is well known that the Glindfeld monastery helped many people in years of famine. Once a year, on Sexagesima Sunday, there was a general distribution of food for the poor children of the town of Medebach. Strangers and tired wayfaring apprentices always found shelter and food in the Glindfeld monastery.

The high altar from the Crosier church at Glindfeld, now in the parish church at Berge, Germany.

We can assume that there was also a guest house in Höhnscheid, not far from Glindfeld.[35] The fifteen-century Crosiers founded an impressive number of new monasteries. As we have already noted, the reformation of the Order was certainly one of the reasons why the nobility, townspeople, and clergy asked the Crosiers to settle near their castles or in their towns. But these Crosiers also remained faithful to their calling as religious ministers; their monastic life was an example to their people, and their liturgy and preaching showed the faithful the way to Christ, especially to Christ crucified. We will return to this subject in our chapter on the spirituality of the Crosiers. Thus far our only purpose has been to make this point: "They know how to make things go. They share with the poor and with everyone." (From the Low German: *"Sie können sich wail behelfen. Sie deilen armen und idermann mit."*)

[35]See A. Grosche, *Geschichte des Klosters Glindfeld* (Bigge, 1958), especially 125-126; A. Van De Pasch, O.S.C., "Het Kruisherenklooster van Glindfeld 1499-1804," *Clairlieu* 10 (1952) 41-53; A. Führer, "Die Pächter des Klosters Glindfeld in den Jahren 1500-1700," *Sauerländer Zeitung* (special edition, 1932-1933) and *Geistliche Nachrichten über Medebach und seine Nachbarorte* (Naumburg, 1938); A. Grosche, *800 Jahre Stadt Medebach* (Medebach, 1951); *Bau- und Kunstdenkmäler von Westfalen* (Münster: Kreis Brilon, 1952) 283-288, 295-324; P. Van Den Bosch, O.S.C., "Winterberg," *Clairlieu* 32 (1974) 77-80; C. F. Padberg, *Küstelberg, Geschichte eines hochsauerländischen Dorfes* (Medebach-Küstelberg, 1975); and Weiss, *Die Kreuzherren in Westfalen*, 177-192, 291-295.

5

The Crosiers in the Sixteenth Century

All religious orders and monasteries experience periods of growth and decline, and the sixteenth century was a period of decline for many of them. If we assume that an order is flourishing when it is expanding and founding new monasteries, we must conclude that the Crosier Order suffered a decline in the sixteenth century, when it ceased to establish new monasteries and lost many of those which had been founded earlier.

The sixteenth century brought many difficulties for the Order, which had to endure attacks both from within and from without. Nevertheless, the Crosiers stood their ground, and despite the suppression of many of their monasteries and the defection of many of their members, their religious life did not fall into decay. Throughout the fifteenth century the Order's general chapters had supported and implemented the Reformation which had begun in 1410 and continued to do so undeviatingly throughout the next century. The Order's leadership remained strong: the priors general at Huy and the definitors responsible for the general chapter were always devout and committed priests and religious.[1]

By the beginning of the sixteenth century, the Crosiers had established many houses in western Europe, and new recruits were flocking in. Influenced by the growing humanism of the time, they increasingly devoted themselves to scholarship. The opportunities

[1]See Van De Pasch, "Het klooster Clairlieu te Hoei," *passim.*

certainly were present: Nikolaas van Haarlem, prior general from 1473 to 1482, urged the priors of all Crosier monasteries to send some of their young confreres to the universities of Paris, Cologne, Toulouse and Caen—cities where Crosier monasteries already existed—for higher studies. In 1491 the Crosiers even founded a monastery in the university city of Louvain for their students.[2]

The monastery at Huy, long a center of scholarship, had a good reputation for theological studies. During the period under consideration here, large numbers of both religious and diocesan clergy came to Huy to attend the theological lectures of Cornelius van Clotingen, O.S.C.

The sixteenth-century high altar from the Crosier at Schwarzenbroich, now in the parish church at Langerwehe, Germany.

[2]See Hermans, *Annales,* 1(1):156, and E. Reussens, "Documents relatifs à l'histoire de l'Université de Louvain, 1425-1797," *Analectes pour servir à l'histoire ecclésiastique de la Belgique* 23 (1892) 212-219.

The new humanism was also making gradual inroads into the life of the monasteries. In Düsseldorf, for example, an unknown Crosier wrote a poem about his monastery's founders, Duke Gerhard and Duchess Sophia. Another Düsseldorf Crosier, Henricus von Gerrisheim, translated the *Vita Swiberti* into German; the translation was printed in Cologne in 1516.[3] Another sign of the times was a change in how the Crosiers referred to themselves. Henceforth they called themselves the *Kreuzherren* (Gentlemen of the Holy Cross) instead of the *Kreuzbrüder* (Brethren of the Holy Cross).

With the spread of printing, Crosier priors sought to acquire scholarly books for their libraries, buying volumes from all over western Europe.[4] But these sixteenth-century Crosiers also continued an art in which they had been engaged for some time: the copying and illumination of manuscripts, chiefly liturgical books, for themselves and others.[5] One of the sixteenth century's most famous miniaturists was Johannes van Deventer, O.S.C., of the monastery of St. Agatha in the Netherlands. He had been trained at the monastery in Cologne, where several such artists were working.[6]

The Crosiers considered their churches to be the very hearts of their monasteries, and during the sixteenth century they happily followed the Counter-Reformation trend of commissioning artists to make altars, statues, and paintings for their churches. The upheaval brought on by the Reformation and the dislocations of the subsequent religious wars often made the annual journey to the general chapters in Huy quite difficult, but whenever the general chapter met, it always addressed the matter of worship in Crosier churches

[3]See Haass, *Die Kreuzherren*, 122-123.

[4]See Van Den Bosch, "De bibliotheken van de Kruisherenkloosters," and "De 500. Verjaring van de boekdrukkunst," *Clairlieu* 34 (1976) 104-108; Van Asseldonk, "Franciscus Vaes van Tongeren"; L. Heere, O.S.C., "Een Maastrichtse bibliofiel prior Jan Proenen," *Clairlieu* 17 (1959) 3-17; and S. Corstens, "Die Anfänge des Kölner Buchdrucks," *Jahrb. d. Köln. Gesch. Vereins* 29-30 (1957) 1-97, and "Die Blütezeit des Kölner Buchdrucks (15.-17. Jahrhundert)," *Rhein. Vierteljahrbl.* 40 (1976) 130-149.

[5]See Kirschbaum, *Liturgische Handschriften* and "Eine Kölner Handschrift des frühen 14. Jahrhunderts," *Beiträge zur rheinischen Kunstgeschichte und Denkmalpflege* 2 (Düsseldorf, 1974) 107-114.

[6]See Van De Pasch, "De drie Gradualia"; see also L. R. Hendriks, "Handschriften van Sint-Agatha," *Brabantia* 6 (1957) 249-265 and "Johannes van Deventer, een bekend miniaturist uit Sint-Agatha," *Numaga* 5 (1958) 78-86.

and always issued directions for a number of modifications. For these chapters, worship was always of primary concern.

Those Crosiers who studied at the various universities found it quite easy to obtain books of questionable orthodoxy, and the general chapters issued frequent warnings against heterodox ideas. The chapter of 1525, for example, forbade Crosiers to join Lutheran sects or to read Luther's works. The general chapter of 1534 also decreed that Crosiers were not to read the works of Desiderius Erasmus, but this decree was later revoked and several monasteries purchased books by Erasmus.[7] Such concerns show us that some Crosiers were in sympathy with Lutheran ideas, and we know that several members of the Order were declared "apostate and fugitive" during the years 1520-1550. The vast majority of Crosiers did not leave their monasteries, however, at least not of their own free choice.

The best-known of those Crosiers who did leave the Order was Gerard Geldenhouwer. He was born at Nijmegen in 1482 and received his elementary education in that same city. In 1492 his father sent him to study the humanities at Deventer, where he boarded with the Brethren of the Common Life and attended the school of Alexander Hegius. Hegius' school was in the vanguard of Dutch humanism and produced a number of well-known humanists. After a number of years, Geldenhouwer decided to enter religious life and become a priest. The Brethren of the Common Life advised him to apply to the Crosier monastery at Asperen. The Asperen Crosiers decided that Geldenhouwer was to complete his higher studies in the humanities and sent him to the Crosier monastery for students in Louvain, where he remained until 1517.

Charles of Austria (later the Emperor Charles V) appointed Geldenhouwer his chaplain in 1514, and thereafter Geldenhouwer also lived in Brussels or in Middelburg, usually in the home of Philip of Burgundy, the admiral of the Flemish fleet, who would later become bishop of Utrecht (1517-1524). Geldenhouwer counted humanists in all three cities among his circle of friends.

Whenever he was in Louvain, he lived in the Crosier monastery there and worked in the printing shop of Dirk Martens, a humanist and friend of Erasmus. Here Geldenhouwer supervised the printing of Erasmus' *Parabolae, sive similium liber et opuscula aliquot* in

[7]See Van Den Bosch, "De bibliotheken van de Kruisherenkloosters," 622.

1515 and Thomas More's *Utopia* in 1518. In 1515 he published his own *Satyrae octo ad verae religionis cultores* from the same shop. This book satirized some theologians in Louvain and criticized certain conditions in the Church; in accord with the ideas of Erasmus, it also defended the study of the Bible and the writings of the Fathers of the Church. During this period Geldenhouwer's faith was quite orthodox, and in 1517 Emperor Maximilian named him poet laureate.

When his master, Philip of Burgundy, became bishop of Utrecht, Geldenhouwer accompanied him as his secretary. It was during these years, he wrote in 1527, that he began to move away from his faith, although he continued to behave in orthodox ways around his friends. During these same years Rome gave him permission to leave the Crosier Order and become a diocesan priest.

After Bishop Philip's death in 1524, Geldenhouwer traveled to Wittenberg and then to Strasbourg. In 1527 his friends learned that he had been deceiving them and living a lie. In a letter from Worms, he told them that he had fallen away from the faith and had married. He was very badly off financially, however, and by the end of that year he returned to the southern Netherlands in extreme poverty, hoping that his friends would help him.

None of them was willing to offer any assistance, however, not even his best friend, Franciscus Cranevelt. Geldenhouwer then returned to Strasbourg, where he lived for some years. There he published some letters which cast suspicion on the orthodoxy of Desiderius Erasmus. The latter was deeply angered and wrote a spirited defense of his Catholic faith, calling Geldenhouwer a lunatic and a Judas.

Geldenhouwer was in Augsburg in 1532. The next year he moved to Marburg to teach history and was appointed a professor at the university there in 1534. He published several more books during his years in Germany, including his best-known work, the *Historia Batavica,* and some biographies of famous Dutch humanists. Gerard Geldenhouwer died of the plague in Marburg on January 10.[8]

We know less about Michel Mulot, prior of the Crosier monastery in Paris from 1521 to 1530. Convinced that the German and Dutch monasteries had too much influence in the governance of the

[8]See O. Hendriks, "Gerardus Geldenhouwer Noviomagus," *Studia Catholica* 31 (1956) 128-149, 176-196.

Order, Mulot and the Paris Crosiers tried to win the independence, of the French Crosiers from the Order's central government. After the Paris "Parlement" removed Mulot from office in 1530, the French Crosiers were reconciled with the prior general, but Mulot moved to Geneva and became a friend and faithful follower of Calvin and Farel.[9]

We have already noted that the Order suffered grievously during the sixteenth century and that the blows came from many different directions.

In Germany, Lutheran rulers drove the Crosiers from Höhnscheid in 1527 and from Osterberg in 1538. The Osterberg Crosiers managed to return to their home but found that orderly monastic life was no longer possible there. Forced to flee again before the advancing Swedes in 1633, they were unable to re-establish themselves in Osterberg a second time. Falkenhagen, another monastery in Westphalia, was suppressed by the Lutherans in 1596.[10]

The year 1538 was a terrible one for the English branch of the Order, too. As part of the campaign against all monastic institutions, King Henry VIII suppressed the Crosier monasteries in his country.

There were also severe losses in the Netherlands during the second half of the sixteenth century. In 1568 a lengthy and protracted war of rebellion broke out between King Philip II of Spain and his Dutch subjects. For the most part, the rebels were Calvinists, and as they widened the territory under their control, more and more Catholics found it difficult to maintain their allegiance to the Pope. By 1596 the Crosiers had been driven from ten of their monasteries and retained only five of their Dutch houses: Venlo, Roermond, Maastricht, St. Agatha, and 's Hertoogenbosch. They continued to reside in three of these—Venlo, Roermond, and Maastricht—only because the Spanish king retained control of those cities. The monastery of St. Agatha, near Cuijk, was under the protection of the House of Orange. Although the members of that noble family were Calvinists and held high offices in the new Republic of the United Netherlands, these lords of Cuijk allowed the Crosiers to remain in

[9]See M. Colson, O.S.C., and J. F. Gilmont, "La carrière mouvementée de Michel Mulot," *Musée Nauchâtelois* (1972) 245–255.

[10]See Weiss, *Die Kreuzherren in Westfalen,* 86–90, 106–116, 174–176.

St. Agatha's.[11] The 's Hertoogenbosch Crosiers, on the other hand, were finally expelled from their city in 1629. After some years of homeless wandering, they were able to settle in Uden, a town situated in the Ravensteijn region, which belonged to the duke of Neuburg.[12]

In the Rhineland, not a single monastery fell victim to the new teachings. One house, that of Pedernach, near Boppard, was closed by the Order itself, since it was too far away from other Crosier communities and had lost a large part of its income when the Reformation had come to Rhens.

These decades of the sixteenth century must have been very difficult for many Crosiers. Some were driven from their homes and work by political and religious strife; more now fell away and abandoned their religious life than had done so in the first half of the century. Every year the general chapter condemned whatever abuses existed in the Order's monasteries and consistently strove to adopt rigorous measures against them. Those Crosiers who remained faithful to their dedication and religious observance carried on very fruitful work, especially in the Rhineland, and successfully preserved the Catholic faith in such places as Beyenburg, Duisburg, Düsseldorf, Marienfrede, Ehrenstein, and Wickrath.[13]

The conditions of the times obviously made it very difficult for these Crosiers to continue their secondary vocation of caring for pilgrims and the needy. The practice of pilgrimage had greatly declined: the religious wars made them impracticable, and many priests preached against them as a perversion of Christianity. The financial resources of the monasteries which cared for pilgrims also suffered seriously because of the Reformation and the wars which followed it. In an effort to cope with their financial difficulties, the Crosiers began to admit a growing number of paying guests, which caused the general chapter of 1593 to decree that priors were not

---

[11]D. Douma, "Het klooster Sint Agatha en de Republiek der Verenigde Nederlanden, 1602-1794," *Merlet, driemaandelijks Blad, streekarchivariaat Land van Cuijk* 7 (1971) 118-132.

[12]See Francino, "Onder Maria's bescherming," 63-98.

[13]See Haass, *Die Kreuzherren,* 18-20, and H. Wamper, *Das Leben der Brüder Adrian und Peter van Walenburch aus Rotterdam und ihr Wirken in der Erzdiözese Köln bis zum Jahre 1649* (Cologne, 1968) 161, 194, 209.

to admit paying guests into their monasteries without the authorization of the prior general and the general chapter.

Nevertheless, the evidence shows that in many places the Crosiers continued to practice hospitality towards those in need, even during these difficult years. As we have already noted, an admirer of the Hohenbusch Crosiers said in 1533, "They know how to make things go. They share with the poor and with everyone." In 1541 the monastery at Brüggen was given a charitable endowment to care for thirty-three people; in 1541 that in Düsseldorf was entrusted with the management of the poorhouses in the Liefergasse; and after the Crosiers of St. Agatha had been temporarily driven from their monastery and were living in Grave, they went on distributing alms to the poor, with the authorization and approval of the city council there.

Unfortunately, the means to help others did not always match the desire. In 1573, for example, the Bentlage Crosiers had to plead that their income was too meager for them to provide food for all the poor who asked for it. There were other instances of a similar willingness to provide whatever help possible, despite the many difficulties which the sixteenth century threw into the path of the Crosier Order.

Our Lady of the Rosary from the Crosier church in Ehrenstein, Germany.

The Glorious Virgin from the Crosier church in Düsseldorf, Germany, now in the Church of St. Lambert in the same city.

6

The Crosiers in the Seventeenth Century

The resolutions of the general chapter of 1609 end with the statement, "such is the race that seeks for him, that seeks the face of the God of Jacob" (Ps 24:6). If we study the resolutions of the general chapters of the seventeenth century, we cannot help but feel that a great change has occurred: the spirit of those who participated in these chapters was quite different from the mood of the preceding century. Sixteenth-century chapters were preoccupied with the negative, for they regularly had to deal with abuses. The chapters of the seventeenth century, on the other hand, were positive. Their instructions to the Crosiers were about how to live as good religious and good Crosiers; their decisions radiated tranquility instead of adversity and disillusionment, and reflect a certainty of what course the Crosiers were to steer by. These chapters were also determined to return to an observance of the old statutes: the dignified recitation of choral prayer, for example, was to be restored in all monasteries as a primary obligation of the Crosiers.

There can be no doubt that the spirit found in the proceedings of these general chapters reflects the spirit dominant in the Order. We can see this, for example, in the ascetic and edifying books published by several Crosiers during the first half of the seventeenth century, such as those by Adam Sasbout of Cologne, Herman von Woestenraedt and Aegidius Colley of Liege, Godefroid van Lith and Theodore Dalenius of Venlo, Jacob Dardeius of Huy, Laurentius

Biel of St. Agatha, and Arnold Hertzworms of Schwarzenbroich (later of Venlo).[1]

Although some of these authors, living as they did in the late Renaissance, occasionally cited ancient Roman writers, most seventeenth-century Crosiers sought inspiration for their religious life in medieval spirituality, probably in reaction to the pervasive influence of humanism.[2] They also made scant use of works by authors of the Counter-Reformation; their sources were the Bible, the Church Fathers, and the important medieval spiritual writers.

Early seventeenth-century pitcher belonging to the Crosier priors of the monastery at Brandenburg.

[1]See Hermans *Annales,* 1(1):239–240, and Vinken, *Spiritualité.*

[2]See Van Den Bosch, "Thomas van Kempen en de Kruisheren," 288–300.

In 1635, for example, Prior General Augustus Neerius (1619–1648) directed Aegidius de Vriese, prior of the monastery at Ehrenstein, to publish the *Vestis Nuptialis (The Wedding Garment),* an ascetic work by Peter Pinchar, a medieval prior general. This book, which had never been printed, was published in 1639 with Neerius' letter of commission as the preface.[3] In the letter, Neerius alludes to the benefits that young Crosiers will derive from the book; both he and de Vriese wanted to impress on the younger men the ideals and the way of life that had marked the medieval Crosiers.

Several Crosiers of the time looked to the history of their Order as an important source of inspiration for their common life. This led to the study of the Order's past and to the publication of books on the subject. We have already mentioned the important chronicle of Henricus Russelius, the prior of Suxy. To his we should add the

An altar antependium from the Crosier church at Glindfeld, now in the city of Hesborn, Germany; a Crosier praying before the Madonna and Christ child.

[3]See chapter 3, note 35; see also A. Van Asseldonk, O.S.C., "Aegidius de Vriese, dichter en leraar aan de Latijnse school te Maaseik," *De Kruisheren te Maaseik* (1955) 114–132, and M. Helin, "Clairlieu au XVIe siècle d'après le 'Journal de Roger de Nimègue,' " *Clairlieu* 9 (1951) 49–66.

names of Pierre Halloix[4] of Liege and Pierre Verduc[5] of Toulouse. Verduc, who called Theodore of Celles a "Knight Hospitaler of the Holy Cross," emphasized even more than Russelius the obligation to help the poor which the founder of the Order imposed on his first confreres. Johannes Banelius of Liege wrote a life of St. Odilia explaining how this saint came to be the Order's patroness.[6] Thomas Franck of Schwarzenbroich wrote the history of his monastery's foundation.[7]

The high altar of the Crosier church in Maaseik, Belgium. The painting, by a member of the school of A. van Dyck, depicts Mary Magdalene and a Crosier, perhaps Theodore of Celles, at the foot of the Cross.

[4]Hermans, *Annales,* 1(1):33.
[5]*Ibid.,* 111.
[6]*Ibid.,* 46.
[7]*Ibid.,* 56.

As we have already mentioned, the general chapter of 1631 reorganized the Order's government with the intention of safeguarding and promoting the movement toward reform. Henceforth the priors general would directly govern only the monasteries in the southern Low Countries; in other areas supervision was placed in the hands of deputies who were at first called "priors provincial" and later "vicars general." Under this arrangement, three new administrative units, each with its own superior, were established: the French province, the Meuse province, and the Rhine province.[8]

The general chapter did not stop with administrative reorganization. Many seventeenth-century Crosiers believed that the slackening of monastic discipline and the defection of numerous members of the Order during the sixteenth century had been mainly due to the superficial formation of young Crosiers. How serious the chapter was about restoring the ideal and the discipline of the Crosiers' common life is evidenced by the printing, for the first time, of the Order's statutes in 1660.[9] For the formation of young Crosiers, the chapter decreed that there should be but one novitiate and one center for philosophical and theological training in each province and that the chapter itself would decide, at every session, in which monasteries these programs would be located. The chapter also emphatically insisted upon the need for study in every monastery and advised the local priors to send talented young Crosiers to the universities. The best of these were selected, by the general chapter, for the Order's programs in philosophy and theology.

There was a further reason for this insistence on the importance of studies. During the first half of the seventeenth century, the Crosiers had begun to devote themselves seriously to the education of youth. This ministry was not entirely new for them: they had already founded Latin schools in Tournai (fifteenth century), Liege (1538), and Wickrath (ca. 1560). But the new century saw the appearance of new schools at Brüggen (1606), Dülken (exact year uncertain), Venlo (1624), St. Agatha (1630), Bitburg (1633), and Maaseik (1644). An attempt to found a school in Düsseldorf failed.

[8]See A. Van De Pasch, O.S.C., "Prior Henricus Walteri Verheyen 1584-1647," *Clairlieu* 32 (1974) 3-74.

[9]The statutes were printed by Peter Metternich of Cologne. For text and comment, see Hermans *Annales,* 3:261-322, and A. Van De Pasch, O.S.C., "Een commentaar op de statuten," *Clairlieu* 7 (1949) 40-53.

In the next century, schools were added in Uden (1743) and Emmerich (1788).

The primary reason for establishing these schools was to provide moral and religious education for young people. The secondary objective was to teach them the Latin language. There were good teachers among the seventeenth-century Crosiers, and several Latin poets, of whom we might note Aegidius de Vriese, Jacob Dardeius, Herman von Woestenraedt, and Theodorus Candidus du Blanc. When Godefroid van Lith published his book *Lucerna Splendens (The Shining Lamp),* his confreres dedicated to him a number of Latin poems (anagrams, epigrams, and chronograms). In keeping with the custom of the time, these tokens of appreciation were all printed in van Lith's book. Latin poetry was, obviously, very popular with the seventeenth-century Crosiers.[10]

During this century the work of the Crosiers continued to expand into other ministries as well, especially the pastoral care of parishes. Such work was not at all foreign to the Order, which had already incorporated the care of several parishes into the apostolic activities of several communities. We know that, among others, the Marienfrede Crosiers had cared for the parish at Loikum, those of Brüggen for Born, those of Schwarzenbroich for Mariaweiler, those of Ehrenstein for Peterslahr, those of Helenenberg for Meckel, those of Glindfeld for Medebach and Winterberg, and those of Scharmer for their local parish and Lütteke Harkstede.

Out of consideration for the wishes of the people they served, Crosier pastors, chaplains, or vicars usually lived outside their monasteries and near the parish churches. The local priors had to get the prior general's authorization for such arrangements, but the permissions were easily obtained, since many parishes would otherwise have been without priests, and the life of the Church would have suffered. These pastors and chaplains were obliged to wear the religious habit and to keep their priors informed about their income and expenditures.

In Germany the Ehrenstein Crosiers were most active in parish work and, during the seventeenth and eighteenth centuries, served parishes in Ehrenstein itself, Peterslahr, Oberlahr, Horhausen, Grossmaischeid, Waldbreitbach, Oberpleis, Aegidienberg, Schlardern, Dattenfeld, Asbach, and Uckerath. The Glindfeld monastery was

[10]See note 2, above.

next, serving Medebach, Winterberg, Küstelberg, Düdinghausen, Eppe, Münden, Oberschledorn, Medelon, Hesborn, Halle, and Dreislar. The Brüggen Crosiers served parishes in Brüggen itself and in Born and Dilkrath. The Helenenberg Crosiers served parishes in Meckel, Esslinger, Bitburg, and Dockendorf; and those of Wickrath the parishes in Wickrath, Borschemich, and Wetschewell. At Duisberg, Wegberg, and Falkenhagen, the local Crosier monastery took responsibility for the local parish. The Beyenburg Crosiers cared for parishes in Beyenburg and Schwelm; those of Hohenbusch for Beeck and Ten Holt. The Cologne monastery cared for the parish at Efferen; that of Schwarzenbroich for Mariaweiler, Geich, and Schevenhütte; that of Marienfrede for Loikum; and that of Bentlage for Salzbergen.

In Dutch-speaking areas, the monastery at St. Agatha cared for Oeffelt, Middellaer, Gennep, Heyen, Beers, and Mook. The Uden Crosiers were pastors at Volkel, Boekel, Orthen, and Overasselt; those of Maastricht at Waltwilder, Haccourt, and Bombaye; those of Maaseik at Heppeneert and Peer; and those of Kolen at Kerniel.

In France, too, the Crosiers staffed a number of parishes.

Although Crosiers were active in the mission to the northern Low Countries, the general chapter was not completely in favor of the Order's involvement in this work, despite the good relations which it enjoyed with Sasbout Vormeer, the apostolic vicar in charge of the mission. (In 1611 Vormeer lived in the Crosier monastery at Emmerich for several months.) Whenever a Crosier was assigned to parish work in the northern Low Countries for several years, his place in that parish could not be taken by another Crosier after he returned to his monastery. We do not know why the general chapter was so cool toward this particular apostolate, but it may have been their wish to spare their Order the sorts of problems encountered by other Orders in the Dutch mission. The Capuchin general chapter, for example, complained that their missionaries working as pastors among the northern Dutch no longer considered themselves bound to the monastic life.

The Rhineland monasteries, Emmerich and Wickrath among others, were especially active in providing Crosiers for the Dutch mission. They served at Duiven, Groessen, Horssen, Oud-Zevenaar, Ulft, Kekerdom, and Weurt in Gelderland; at Wervershoef, Bovenkarpsel, Westerblokker, Spanbroek, and Weesp in North Holland; at Utrecht, Leusden, and Amersfoort in Utrecht; at Ooster-wierum in Groningen; and at Dordrecht and Raamburg in South Holland. In all these parishes the Crosiers worked as pastors or curates to preserve and deepen the Catholic faith. They met with considerable success, and, in many cases, brought about a revival of the people's faith.[11]

In all the parishes they cared for, the Crosiers were especially concerned to promote confraternities, pious associations intended to deepen the religious life of their members and to help the needy. In almost every one of their monastery or parish churches, the Crosiers established one or two of these associations; the most common were the Confraternity of the Holy Cross and the Confraternity of the Holy Trinity. (The latter was originally founded by the Trinitarians, an order with whom the Crosiers may have felt some kinship: the Trinitarians wore a red-and-blue cross and were sometimes called Crosiers, too. Originally their confraternities raised funds to help ransom enslaved Christians; later they collected alms to educate poor children in Asia and Africa.)

In many parishes the Crosiers also founded Confraternities of the Holy Rosary. In 1516 Pope Leo X had granted the Order's prior general the faculty of blessing rosaries with a special indulgence which, until modern times, was known as the Crosier Indulgence.[12]

Did these seventeenth-century Crosiers do much for the needy beyond founding confraternities? Did they continue their traditional secondary vocation of helping the poor and pilgrims? We do know that their schools often sponsored students whose parents could not afford the school fees, which was another way to help the poor and the needy. And as we have already said, the Helenenberg Crosiers were asked to take over a hospice in Bitburg in 1633, which is surely a testimony to their reputation.

The unremitting wars which swept over Europe throughout the seventeenth and eighteenth centuries made it impossible for pilgrims to travel any distance. Fewer pilgrims were on the roads which passed the monasteries, so the Crosiers opened their guest houses, for a fee,

[11]See L. Emond, O.S.C., *Kruisheren-missionarissen in de Nederlanden* (Cuijk: St. Agatha, 1933), and L. Heere, O.S.C., "Een Hollands College ten Cruycenbroederen tot Colen," *Clairlieu* 7 (1949) 101–108.

[12]See A. Ramaekers, O.S.C., "De Kruisherenaflaat," *Clairlieu* 6 (1948) 3–52.

to people who would be staying in a given locality for some time—a practice which had started in the preceding century.

But if the number of pilgrims journeying to remote places declined, the local pilgrimage still remained popular, and Crosier churches attracted significant numbers of people from nearby neighborhoods. During this period, several of the churches laid great emphasis on the veneration of the Mother of God: those, for example, at Namur, Dinant, Brüggen, Düsseldorf, Ehrenstein, Venlo, Heppeneert (near Maaseik), and Uden. In 1674 the Crosiers of Uden were assigned the care of a chapel in which Our Lady of the Linden was venerated. This local devotion had been quiescent throughout the seventeenth century, but revived under the direction and encouragement of the Crosiers. Until the beginning of the nineteenth century, seventy large groups of pilgrims came to Uden every year to ask the intercession of Our Lady of the Linden.[13] We may assume that large crowds also flocked to the other churches mentioned above in which the Mother of God was venerated.

Somewhat smaller numbers of pilgrims came to venerate the relics of St. Odilia, the patron saint of the Crosiers, in the churches of Huy, Liege, and Brandenburg. The same is true of the cult of St. Matthias at Schwarzenbroich and of St. Languida and St. Leonard at Tournai.

During the seventeenth and eighteenth centuries, then, the care of pilgrims continued to be an important part of the Crosiers' work, as it had been in the Middle Ages. Where pilgrims come, the poor come, too, and this required the Crosiers to care for the indigent as well as for travelers. We know that in Namur, for instance, the Crosiers distributed bread to the poor every day, and that the prior of St. Agatha could claim that his monastery had never been without its poor. Such must have been the case in all Crosier monasteries, especially those where pilgrims visited the churches.

Economically, the seventeenth century began badly for the Crosier monasteries. The Rhineland monasteries, for example, suffered much from the Thirty Years' War. Things did improve, however, later in the century. The monasteries of Beyenburg, Ehrenstein, and Helenenberg, which had been completely sacked earlier, were able

[13]See Francino, "Onder Maria's bescherming," 77–86.

to equip their churches with baroque altars, pulpits, and choir stalls. Other Rhineland churches were renovated, too, and acquired valuable pieces to adorn their interiors. In this the Crosiers continued their tradition of furnishing their churches as richly as possible. Some of these furnishings were of their own workmanship, for there had always been artists among the Crosiers. A workshop in the Aachen monastery, for example, produced artistic wood carvings,[14] and the Namur Crosier Herman Pietkin built organs for the monastery churches at Huy, Maastricht, Düsseldorf, Tournai, Namur, and Liege, and for the church of St. Adalbert in Aachen, among others.[15]

In 1675, the archbishop of Cologne, Maximilian Heinrich von Bayern (1650–1688), sent Rome a very favorable report on the Crosiers. He praised their piety, their zeal in preaching, and their success in preserving the Catholic faith. He also noted their dedication to scholarship and to the education of the young. Some of these Crosiers held the degree of master of arts and were professors at the University of Cologne.[16]

Compared with the preceding century, the seventeenth was a prosperous time for the Order, even though only one monastery (Wegberg) was founded during the entire period.[17] No one could have guessed that, within another hundred years, the Crosier Order would almost be dead.

---

[14]See Haass, *Die Kreuzherren,* 112, and *Führer durch Heilige-Kreuz-Kirche in Aachen,* passim.

[15]See *Clairlieu* 17 (1959) 57.

[16]See Haass, *Die Kreuzherren,* 32.

[17]See *ibid.,* 225–232; see also G. Evertz, "Pastor Sibenius, der Kreuzherr und religiöse Eiferer im und nach dem dreissigjährigen Krieg," *Clairlieu* 17 (1959) 18–25, and *Kirchengeschichte der Pfarre Wegberg* (Wegberg, 1977).

7

The Enlightenment

The eighteenth century was a sad time for the Crosier Order, sadder even than the sixteenth century had been. To use an old metaphor, the ship of the Order sailed on a very stormy sea which battered it from every side. Had all the crew cooperated, a clever and experienced captain might have brought the severely damaged vessel into port. Instead, the ship drifted out of control and eventually struck a rock. Through divine providence, the Order did not go under: the ship was lost, but the crew escaped.

Although it may seem severe, our judgment is that responsibility for the wreckage of the Order at the end of the eighteenth century can be determined. One of the most important causes, if not the decisive one, was discord within the Order—a lack of collaboration among the Crosiers. This is not to brand them mutineers or rebels; they simply had not given enough thought to their life as Crosiers. Had they known how dangerous the seas were becoming, they might have better prepared themselves for the voyage.

In the Middle Ages the general chapter had been a meeting of the priors and some members of all Crosier monasteries, who together considered the interests and the concerns of the Order and together formulated the resolutions of each chapter. Unfortunately, the general chapter did not meet regularly during the eighteenth century, and not at all between 1698 and 1715 or between 1739 and 1749, when the Wars of the Spanish and Austrian Successions (1701–1714 and 1740–1748, respectively) kept Crosiers from traveling to Huy.

In 1773 a decision was made to hold the general chapter every sixth year, but subsequent chapters met only in 1779 and 1786. (The chapters held in the three Crosier "provinces" had ceased meeting in 1682.)

The reasons for the infrequent meetings of the chapter were manifold, of course. Priors complained that the journey to Huy was too expensive, forgetting that the annual trip to the motherhouse had been much more difficult for their medieval predecessors. The real reason for their resistance probably was a growing desire for autonomy in the local houses, that is, for a greater measure of independence from the prior general and other monasteries. The rationalist and Febronian ideas fashionable during the eighteenth century certainly played some part in shaping this attitude but so did the autocratic attitude adopted by several priors general at Huy.

In 1630 the priors general had received the *pontificalia*—the right to administer the minor orders and to display some of the appurtenances of a bishop. Not only did they wear a purple mozetta (a short cape), a pectoral cross and a ring, but also adopted coats of arms, began making greater and greater use of a personal seal, and started having their portraits painted. They even owned a private villa (le château de Lamalle) on the left bank of the Meuse, six miles from Huy. The vicars they appointed for the Rhine and Meuse provinces were regarded as little more than spies who kept the prior general informed about whatever was going on.

On the other hand, many local Crosier priors assumed the status of high prelates and arrogated to themselves all sorts of privileges, such as reserving a part of the monastery as their private quarters. Prior Rudolph Lafarth of Glindfeld and Prior Mathias Goffins of Liege were both protonotaries (high dignitaries) of the Apostolic See.

In 1765 a violent quarrel broke out between Prior General Lambert de Fisen (1741–1778) and several priors. The War of the Austrian Succession had kept de Fisen from convoking his first general chapter until 1749. When that chapter assembled, de Fisen submitted to it a set of new statutes which had been drafted by Henricus Seulen, prior of Liege. They apparently met with little enthusiasm, since the prior general re-submitted them to each of the next three Chapters (1752, 1756 and 1764). During the 1764 chapter he simply told the priors to study the statutes as drafted and to send their observations within a fortnight to two of the definitors. The latter were to review the priors' observations and draft a set of amended statutes, which would be submitted to the prior general for publication. In 1765 Prior General de Fisen had these statutes-as-amended printed and promulgated, imposing them on all Crosiers. Most of the priors from the Rhine and Meuse provinces took strong exception. Their main objections were that the prior general had forced the statutes on the Order without proper authorization by the general chapter and without following traditional practice, which required the approval of three general chapters; and that these new statutes, which significantly curtailed the power of priors, would make the general chapter subordinate to the prior general.

Some animosity on the part of the German and Dutch houses toward the French monasteries, who supported the prior general's action, may have encouraged the quarrel. At any rate, it went on for three years, until Rome ruled in favor of the protesting priors in 1768.[1]

This growing spirit of autonomy also undermined the earlier practice of a common novitiate and common house of philosophical and theological studies. In 1733 at least fourteen monasteries were providing such education to their young members; inevitably, this dispersion of resources led to results which can described as not uniformly good. Prior General Johannes Reynders (1735-1741) tried, with some success, to centralize education once more. Education improved in some of the monasteries: at Huy, Hohenbusch, and St. Agatha, and other monasteries, young Crosiers defended theological theses in the same way university students did.[2]

Only a small number of authors appeared among the Crosiers during the eighteenth century. Worthy of note are the philosopher Lambert de Fisen,[3] the Church historian Gerard Casteel of Duisburg,[4]

---

[1]See E. Fontaine, O.S.C., "Une première crise à Clairlieu au XVIIIe siècle, 1735-1752," *Clairlieu* 8 (1950) 3-30; L. Heere, O.S.C., "Dokumenten uit de statutenstrijd van 1765," *Clairlieu* 18 (1960) 71-80; and A. Van De Pasch, O.S.C., "Kapittelbesluiten van het Kruisherenklooster te Keulen 1679-1789," *Clairlieu* 33 (1975) 31-58.

[2]See Hermans *Annales,* 1(2):125-126, 133-135, 138, 160.

[3]See Th. Huybers, O.S.C., "Een philosophische cursus van Kruisheer L. de Fisen, 1728-1729," *Clairlieu* 10 (1952) 3-26.

[4]See Hermans *Annales,* 1(2):120; Haass, *Die Kreuzherren,* 44-53; and Van Den Bosch, "Thomas van Kempen en de Kruisheren," 302-303.

the moral theologain Henricus Seulen of Liege,[5] and Jacob Hoogen of Wegberg. Hoogen, who came on the scene late in the century, was a Crosier of considerable importance.

Hoogen stood among the first rank of enlightened Catholic clerics of the lower Rhine at the end of the eighteenth and beginning of the nineteenth century. A simple country pastor without scholarly airs, he exerted an influence in German lands far beyond his native Rhineland through his activity, his writings, and his far-reaching connections with like-minded theologians, pedagogues and statesmen. He influenced both Catholic and Evangelical circles, and received recognition from both friends and foes in those troubled times.[6]

Jacob Hoogen attended the famous Gymnasium Laurentianum in Cologne. In 1760, at the age of eighteen, he received the degree of master of arts, and at twenty became a professor in his former school. He entered the Crosier Order in 1767—at which monastery, we do not know. Two years later he became a curate and teacher in Wegberg, and at age twenty-nine became prior and pastor there. After the Napoleonic suppression of the monastery in 1802, Hoogen lived with his brother in Aldekerk, where he died in 1805.

Hoogen strove for a deepening and personalizing of the Christian religion; he decried superstition and the abuses and scandals connected with pilgrimages and indulgences. Believing that a good educational system would eliminate poverty,[7] he promoted a thorough reformation of schools and religious instruction. Although many of his attitudes reflect the cosmopolitanism and tolerance fashionable in his time, Hoogen was deeply committed to Jesus as

---

[5]See Hermans, *Annales,* 1(2):143, and Van Den Bosch, "Thomas van Kempen en de Kruisheren," 301–302.

[6]W. Zimmermann, "Jakob Hoogen (1742–1805), Prior des Kreuzherrenklosters und Pfarrer in Wegberg, der führende Aufklärer und Pädagoge am Neiderrhein," *Rhein. Vierteljahrsbl.* 19 (1954) 227–248. See also R. Haass, "Jakob Hoogen," *Clairlieu* 10 (1952) 54–62, and "Prior Jakob Hoogen, ein führender Kopf der Aufklärung am Niederrhein," *Annalen des historischen Vereins für dem Niederrhein* 128 (1956) 210–225.

[7]See Haass, "Prior Jakob Hoogen," 221–224.

the Way, the Truth, and the Life. He wrote nine books and a large number of treatises, the proceeds from several of which he designated for the assistance of poor children in the schools. In this, he was a Crosier true to the ancient ideal of his Order: helping the poor.

Although we do not know whether Jacob Hoogen found kindred spirits among his confreres, we do know that the eighteenth-century Crosiers continued operating their Latin schools. The Emmerich Crosiers, for example, took over the *Gymnasium* (the rough equivalent of a high school) in their city in 1788.[8] And throughout the century the Crosiers continued their parish ministry, too.

Consideration of the Crosiers' manifold pastoral activities makes it impossible to avoid the question of whether or not the Order's monastic discipline really slackened during this period. Works which relate the history of individual houses suggest that such often was the case.

The 1765 edition of the Order's statutes suggest that eighteenth-century Crosiers lived quite differently from their seventeenth-century predecessors. These statutes were adapted to the contemporary practices of the Crosiers and were more liberal than previous codes had been. The resolutions of the general chapters also reveal the existence of abuses in some Crosier monasteries. The campaigns for autonomy waged by certain priors had probably not benefited monastic discipline, and some enlightened Crosiers may have concluded that monasteries were no longer relevant. Unfortunately, we do not have sufficient information to form a clear picture of the Crosiers' way of life in the eighteenth century. We do know that they did not share common goals and did not cooperate with each other.

The internal situation was further complicated by outside interference. Archbishop Maximilian of Cologne (1784–1801), an Austrian and an enlightened despot, forbade the Crosiers in his city to attend the general chapter of 1786 and denied the prior general the right to officially visit Crosier monasteries in his archdiocese.[9] The archbishop's older brother was Emperor Joseph II, who imitated his brother's example by forbidding those Crosiers living in the Austrian Netherlands to have any contact with the prior general on the

[8] See *Emmerich* (1952), 4–52.

[9] See Haas, *Die Kreuzherren*, 40–41.

grounds that the head of the Order lived in Liege, a "foreign country" ruled by a prince-bishop.[10]

Despite their problems, nearly all the Crosiers remained loyal to the Church and, after the suppression of their monasteries, continued to work as pastors.[11] Only one Crosier is known to have left the Order in the late eighteenth century, and that was Matthias Biergans of Schwarzenbroich, who later railed against the Church and clergy and against the Bible and Christianity in *Brutus,* a contemporary review.[12]

As the ideas of the Enlightenment spread ever more widely in the second half of the eighteenth century, antipathy toward the Church in general and toward monasteries in particular kept increasing. Young people pulled back from entering the religious life, and the Order found fewer recruits.[13]

Whatever internal problems the Crosier Order suffered, the real reason for its serious, though temporary, decline during this period was an external one, namely, the desire of enlightened despots, large and small, to wipe religious orders out of existence.

The campaign against the Crosiers opened in France, where the Order had twelve foundations, and in the Austrian Netherlands. King Louis XV of France suppressed most of the monasteries there because, in his opinion, they had not lived up to their program of reform. The Paris monastery still existed in 1790, but disappeared shortly thereafter. Claiming that they were no longer of any use to the people, Emperor Joseph II closed the monasteries at Namur (1779) and at Roermond, Tournai, and Brandenburg (1783) in the Austrian Netherlands.

The French revolutionary army conquered the Austrian Netherlands and the Princedom of Liege in 1795 and invaded the Rhineland. All monasteries in the occupied areas were closed forthwith, including the Crosier houses at Huy, Liege, Dinant, Kerniel, Carignan, Suxy, Virton, Maaseik, Maastricht, Venlo, and Düsseldorf. This was followed, in 1802, by Napoleon's suppression of all monasteries on

---

[10]See E. Fontaine, O.S.C., "Mgr. Jacques Dubois, Général des PP. Croisiers à Huy, 1778-1796," *Clairlieu* 4-5 (1946-1947) 1-223.

[11]Husman and Trippel, *Geschichte der ehemaligen Herrlichkeit,* 109.

[12]See Haas, *Die Kreuzherren,* 103-104.

[13]See A. Deblon, "Les croisiers ordonnés à Liège aux 17ᵉ et 18ᵉ siècles," *Clairlieu* 33 (1975) 59-78.

the left bank of the Rhine, which ended the Crosier foundations at Cologne, Schwarzenbroich, Brüggen, Dülken, Wickrath, Aix-la-Chapelle (Aachen), Helenenberg, and Wegberg. A year later the German princes, through the *Reichsdeputationshauptschluss*, claimed control over all monasteries. Under this act, the first Crosier monasteries to be closed were Beyenburg and Glindfeld (1804), followed by Emmerich (1811), Marienfrede and Ehrenstein (1812), and finally Duisburg (1814). When the process ended, forty-four Crosier monasteries had been suppressed, leaving only those at St. Agatha and Uden, both in the Netherlands.[14]

A heavy cross was thus laid upon the Order once more. The Crosiers were able to retain their last two monasteries throughout Napoleon's rule and into the reign of King William I (1813–1840). William decreed that both should die. But God disposed otherwise. Remarkably, these two monasteries, whose existence had been continuously threatened since the sixteenth century and who had been forced to bear Christ's Cross of suffering continuously, were chosen to save the Order of the Holy Cross.

[14]See Fontaine, "Jacques Dubois," *passim;* and, by the same author, "Les Croisiers de Liège en face de la suppression 1796," *Clairlieu* 7 (1949) 14–39; "La fin du prieuré de Carignan"; "La fin de Clairlieu," *Clairlieu* 9 (1951) 6–42; and "Le definitoire, 1796–1802," *Clairlieu* 10 (1952) 28–36. See also M. Colson, O.S.C., "De Kruisheren van Venlo tijdens de Franse Revolutie," *Clairlieu* 13 (1956) 49–89 and 14 (1957) 3–59; R. Büttner, *Die Säkularisation der Kölner geistlichen Institutionen* (Cologne, 1971); W. Klompen, *Die Säkularisation im Arrondissement Krefeld* (Kempen, 1962) passim; and G. Evertz, *Die Zeit der Französischen Fremdherrschaft, 1794–1814, in der Gemeinde Wegberg* (Wegberg, 1960).

8

Crosier Spirituality[1]

Until now we have concerned ourselves with tracing the history of the Crosiers from around 1210 to 1812. Whatever their shortcomings during these centuries, they did seek God. They found man, very often the poor man.

The Crosiers lived as every follower of Christ did. They went to church to pray. They asked God the Father to make his will clear; they asked God the Son and God the Holy Spirit for what was needed to carry out that will: they asked the Son for the grace and strength he had won for all people on the Cross; they asked the Holy Spirit for wisdom and insight.

They considered Jesus the model to be imitated in their own lives. They were aware of the needs of other people and, Christ-like, tried to help them to the best of their ability. They were often weak, too, and sought forgiveness in the sacrament of confession before they felt worthy to receive communion. They honored God and begged for their daily bread in the Lord's Prayer; they honored the Mother of God and prayed the Hail Mary for her help. They looked to the saints for examples of Christian living and sought their intercession in time of need. They wished to come to the end of their lives at

[1]See especially M. Vinken, O.S.C., *The Spirituality of the Crosier Fathers*, trans. B. Van Gils, O.S.C. (Syracuse Ind, 1957) and *Spiritualité*, cols. 2574–2575; *Lectures on Crosier Spirituality*, trans. F. Jutte, O.S.C. and others (Fort Wayne, Ind, 1957); *Inhoud en waarde van regel en constituties der Kruisheren* (Diest, 1957); and Van De Ven, "Kruisheren."

A Crosier venerates the body of Christ taken down from the Cross; from a seventeenth-century engraving.

peace with God, so as to love him forever and rise one day as Christ did.

The Crosiers lived as the members of any other religious order did. Seeking a special bond with God, they proposed a radical imitation of Christ. They took three vows: the vow of obedience because, like Christ, they chose to serve rather than to dominate; the vow of chastity because they wanted to be open to all rather than caught in a net of personal obligations; the vow of poverty because they wished to be generous rather than possessive.

Accepting one of their own as leader, they lived together under one roof because they were seeking more than personal betterment:

they wanted each other's sanctification. They prayed together. Because they sometimes fell short of their ideals, they were urged to live ascetically, imitating Christ, as the great saints had done, in fasting and penance. They were to lead a contemplative life, observing silence in the monastery; they were to read the Bible and reflect on it. The Crosiers lived as all other canons regular did. Prayer was important to them. The Scriptures had taught the Jewish people to pray without ceasing; Jesus, too, often retired to pray alone to his heavenly Father and taught his disciples to do the same. From the first centuries of Christianity, monks prayed to God several times each day, using the psalms of the Old Testament. Because the monks chanted these prayers together, this form of worship was later called choral prayer. Like many monks and secular canons (priests attached to a cathedral church), canons regular pledged themselves to choral prayer; in this prayer, scheduled for several times each day, they praised God and asked him to help all people to happiness.[2]

But canons regular had special characteristics of their own. Unlike secular canons, they chose membership in a religious order. Unlike monks, they chose to dedicate themselves to the pastoral care of the people, as the mendicants did, but unlike mendicants, their monasteries were allowed to own property. Another point of difference between them and the mendicants, who traveled throughout Europe preaching the Gospel, was that canons regular proposed to work only from their own monastery and church, serving the people in their immediate neighborhood and those who came to them, as recommended by St. Augustine, whose Rule they followed. They singled out for special concern the poor, the sick, and passing pilgrims. They used the income from their common property to build hospices and guest houses for these people and gave them food and drink, as Christ had commanded: "For I was hungry and you gave me food. I was thirsty and you gave me drink, I was a stranger and you welcomed me, naked and you clothed me. I was ill and you comforted me. . . ." (Matt 25:35-36).

---

[2]See H. Van Rooijen, O.S.C., "Kruisheren," *Liturgisch Woordenboek* (Roermond-Maaseik, 1958-67) 2, cols. 1397-1405, and "The Liturgy of the Crosiers," *Crosier Heritage* 10 (September, 1983) 1-6; A. Van Asseldonk, O.S.C., "Het Brevier van de Kruisheren," *Clairlieu* 3 (1944) 8-144; G. A. Meijer, "Een Ordinarium der Kruisheren," *Archief voor de Geschiedenis van het Aartsbisdom Utrecht* 41 (1915) 97-194; and L. Heere, O.S.C., "De oude gebruiken."

Like other religious orders, canons regular did not always live up to their ideals. Whenever they undertook reform, they realized that their efforts to live a common life required a meaning, a goal. They always rediscovered this meaning, this goal, in helping the needy; once again, they shared with everyone.

The Crosiers' lives, then, were similar to those of every Christian, every member of a religious order, and every canon regular. But was there anything special, anything particularly characteristic of the Crosiers which distinguished them from other clergy and other canons regular?

On the surface one could point to their distinctive habit, on which they wore that conspicuous red-and-white cross. They also painted or carved their cross over the entrances of their monasteries and churches and on the walls and ceilings of their churches, chapter rooms, and refectories. The Order's motto was, and is, *"in Cruce salus"* (in the Cross is salvation). Was this only a motto, or was the Cross truly significant in the life of the Crosiers?

The Apostle Peter wrote, "It was for this you were called, since Christ suffered for you in just this way and left you an example, to have you follow in his footsteps" (1 Pet 2:21). The Crosiers certainly intended to follow in the steps of the suffering Christ.[3] Their spirituality, which was based on prayer, especially on choral prayer, focused on Christ's suffering from the *mandatum* (his washing of the disciples' feet at the Last Supper) to his death on the cross. The ascetical authors among the Crosiers urged their confreres to ponder the whole way of the Cross during the hours of choral prayer. Every Thursday or Friday evening, as we have already noted, the prior was to wash the feet of his confreres, as Christ had done at the Last Supper. Each day at noon (later at three in the afternoon), a bell was rung to remind the Crosiers to prayerfully recall Christ's suffering and death.

Their major liturgical celebrations were Good Friday and the feasts of the Finding of the Cross (May 3) and the Exaltation of the Cross (September 14). They composed some beautiful sequences for these feasts, and on those days marched in procession outside of their churches. On the Fridays when no saint's feast was celebrated, the

[3] See J. Van Den Bosch, O.S.C., "De H. Kruis- en Passiecultus in het geestlijk leven der Kruisbroeders," *Cruciferana* n.s. 7 (1942).

Crosiers prayed the *Officium Crucis* (the Office of the Cross) and frequently added a *commemoratio Sanctae Crucis* (commemoration of the Holy Cross) to the end of Lauds. As early as the beginning of the sixteenth century, the Crosiers were praying special forms of the Divine Office for feasts of the Sacred Crown of Thorns, the Holy Lance and Nails, and the Holy Shroud.

During the Middle Ages Crosiers had composed many beautiful prayers commemorating the Cross and Christ's suffering,[4] prayers which reveal a deep veneration for the Heart of Jesus. A statue in the monastery church of Ehrenstein bears witness to this devotion. It portrays the Risen Christ; in his left hand he carries a banner displaying a cross, and with his right he points to the wound in his side from which flows a stream of blood. Medieval Crosiers claimed that their red-and-white cross symbolized the blood and water which streamed from Christ's side when it was pierced by a soldier after his death. Later, monasteries and priors would use the heart of Christ in their coats of arms. In this they were continuing a traditional motif, for the Crosiers had always represented their spiritual father, St. Augustine, by means of a heart aflame with love.

These are only a few examples of the Crosiers' spiritual orientation. We may safely assume that many Crosiers used the prayers composed by their confreres for their private devotions outside the assigned hours of choral prayer. On the other hand, we know that members of the Order were obliged to pray the Stations of the Cross for deceased confreres and that, at some Crosier monasteries, a Way of the Cross was erected outside, as was the case at Glindfeld and Schwarzenbroich and perhaps also at Ehrenstein.

One thing is certain: the Crosiers distinguished themselves from other religious orders and other communities of canons regular by their special veneration of the Cross. This veneration manifested itself in other ways than liturgies and prayers commemorating the Cross and Christ's suffering. Crosiers promoted it in books and ser-

[4]See Vinken, *Spirituality of the Crosier Fathers,* 49–59; K. Richstätter, *Altdeutsche heilige Stunde zu Ehren des heiligsten Herzens Jesu* (Munich, 1938); A. Van Asseldonk, O.S.C., "Middelleeuwse gebeden in Udens 16e eeuwse Brevier," *Clairlieu* 12 (1954) 17–38; L. Heere, O.S.C., "Matthijs Brouwers, Een excellente oeffinghe van het lijden ende passie O.H.J.C. ende wordt genaemt het cruysgebet," *Clairlieu* 18 (1960) 86–87; A. Van De Pasch, O.S.C., "Uit een Devotieboekje van de vroegere Klaaskerk te Venlo," *Clairlieu* 34 (1976) 3–10; and the *Hymnarium Sanctae Agathae.*

mons emphasizing this theme and by enthusiastically establishing Confraternities of the Holy Cross in their churches in order to foster the veneration of the Cross among the people. Crosier veneration of the Cross also produced a specific asceticism and theology of the Cross. The Order's ascetical writers continuously emphasized the obligation they and and their confreres had to live out the way of the Cross, in accord with St. Peter's directive. Everyone must carry the cross, but the Crosiers were to give other Christians an example of resignation and renunciation by being real cross-bearers.

In Crosier theology, the Cross is the sign of victory: a tree bearing abundant fruit, a ladder for sinners, a remedy for physical and spiritual illnesses, a heavenly pearl, the gate of heaven, a comfort for those who grieve. Crosier liturgical texts are rich in such metaphors, echoing the themes of joy and gratitude. At the beginning of the High Mass on the feast of the Exaltation of the Cross, the Crosiers sang an *introit* text which is a short but sublime summation of their theology of the Cross: "We ought to glory in the Cross of our Lord, Jesus Christ; in whom is our salvation, our life, and resurrection, and by whom we are saved and set free."[5]

Beside the Cross on Calvary stood Mary, the Mother of Jesus. As we have already mentioned, in the seventeenth and eighteenth centuries many Crosier churches fostered a growing devotion to Mary, a devotion which the Crosiers had long shared.[6] Since 1248 their formula for the profession of vows had included a pledge of obedience to God *and* to Mary. In addition to the celebrations of Mary in the universal calendar of the Church, the Crosiers observed a whole series of Marian feasts: the Compassion of the Blessed Virgin Mary (changed to the feast of the "Seven Sorrows of Mary" at the end of the seventeenth century), the Conception, the Joys, and the Hope of the Blessed Virgin Mary. The numerous books about Mary which the Crosiers copied during the fifteenth century bear further witness to their devotion to her. They also had always promoted the devotion of the rosary: in 1516 Pope Leo X granted

[5]Nos autem gloriari oportet in Cruce Domini nostri Jesu Christi; in quo est salus, vita et resurrectio; per quem salvati et liberati sumus.

[6]See L. Emond, O.S.C., "De Maria-cultus in de Orde van het H. Kruis," *Ons Geestelijk Erf* 1 (1927) 49–55; Vinken, *Spiritualité*, 59–63, and "Le culte marial chez les Croisiers," *Maria, études sur la sainte Vierge* (Paris, 1949); and Van Den Bosch, "Düsseldorf."

the faithful who prayed the Lord's Prayer or the Hail Mary on a rosary blessed by the prior general of the Crosiers an indulgence of five hundred days.

Did the Crosiers have a special devotion to the Sorrowful Mother? This is an important question, and evidence of such a devotion does exist. In the churches at Ehrenstein and Beyenburg, both now cared for by the Crosiers once more, special devotion to the Sorrowful Mother has survived to the present. Prior General Georgius Constantini (1587–1602) directed the Crosiers to sing the antiphon *Haec est praeclarum vas* ("This is the glorious vessel") every Saturday; in it they invoked Mary's assistance in time of plague. Later they sang this antiphon every day, always concluding, as the custom had been from the first, with a prayer to the Sorrowful Mother. When they prayed the Litany of Our Lady after Compline in the evening, they often added the prayer to the Sorrowful Mother.[7]

Evidence from the first centuries of the Order is too scant, however, to warrant the conclusion that the earliest Crosiers had a special devotion to the Sorrowful Mother. Some prayer books from the fifteenth century do contain an office of the Sorrowful Mother, but it is possible that these were for private use only.[8]

The Crosiers did favor certain saints, too, as is apparent from the consecration or the dedication of the altars, and the statues and paintings in the earlier Crosier churches.

Foremost among the saints they venerated were St. Helena and St. Quiriacus, for tradition claimed that these saints had found the cross of Christ and had founded an Order of the Holy Cross in the fourth century.

From 1287 on, the Crosiers especially venerated St. Odilia, one of the companions of St. Ursula, all of whom were martyred in Cologne by the Huns. The Order's tradition has it that, in 1287, a Crosier brother in Paris was directed to exhume the relics of St. Odilia in Cologne and bring them to the Crosier monastery in Huy, for she was to be the patron saint of the Crosier Order. When the relics were transferred to Huy that year, they were placed in a wooden reliquary. A contemporary artist decorated its exterior with scenes

[7]See L. Heere, O.S.C., "Een Nederlands Antifoon," *Ons Geestlijk Erf* 26 (1952) 105–112.

[8]See Vinken, *Spirituality of the Crosier Fathers*, 61–62.

The discovery of the relics of St. Odilia; from an altar antependium from the Crosier church in Beyenburg, Germany.

from the the saint's life and the transfer of her relics. The reliquary is presently kept in the former Crosier monastery at Kerniel, Belgium; the scenes on its exterior are among the oldest wood-panel paintings in northwestern Europe. The paintings on the reliquary suggest that the thirteenth-century Crosiers saw the transfer of the saint's relics from Cologne to Huy as heaven's approval of their loving service of the needy. Legend says that, when St. Odilia appeared to Brother John in Paris, she was carrying a banner displaying a red-and-white cross. For centuries, then, the Crosiers have chosen to portray their patron saint in this way. Consequently, we believe that they considered the banner the saint's encouragement to continue their works of service under her protection and as a promise that their work would bear fruit. They certainly must have been pleased, too, to know that a holy pilgrim had become their patron saint. (Legend said that Odilia had been on a pilgrimage to Rome from her home in Britain when she was martyred.)[9]

After 1287 the Crosier church in Huy became a pilgrimage center, as the Crosiers quite understandably promoted devotion to their

[9]See L. Honhon, O.S.C., *De heilige Odilia, maagd en martelares, Patrones van de orde der Kruisheren* (Roermond, 1887); H. Van Lieshout, O.S.C., *Rond het reliekschrijn van Sint Odilia* (Hasselt, 1935); Van Rooijen, *Sinte Odilia;* B. Mischke, O.S.C., *Odilia, Maid of the Cross* (Onamia, MN, 1955); Van Asseldonk, "Handschriften van Kruisheren"; L. Roppe, A. Dusar, and M. Colson, O.S.C., *Het Odiliaschrijn, Klooster Kolen-Kerniel* (Hasselt, 1965).

own patroness. Later (we are uncertain of the date) people began invoking the help of St. Odilia in healing diseases of the eyes; pilgrims to Huy touched their eyes with water blessed in honor of St. Odilia.

But these three patronal saints were not the only ones whom the Crosiers honored. We have already pointed out that many Crosier churches were dedicated to "hospice saints" and the patrons of pilgrims. In these churches, the Crosiers promoted not only the veneration of the local patron, but of other hospice or pilgrim saints, too. In the Crosier church at Aix (Aachen), for example, there was veneration of Sts. Sebastian, George, and Egidius as well as of St. Julian.

A saint venerated in all Crosier churches was Mary Magdalene, as we know from statues and paintings which have survived and from liturgical directions. Like those of St. Helena and St. Odilia, the feast of St. Mary Magdalene was *totum duplex* and a "prioral" feast, which means that the prior led the Divine Office and was the celebrant of the community's High Mass. (In 1727 the feast became "subprioral.")[10]

To explain the Crosiers' special veneration for this saint, we must turn again to the Order's spirituality.

Mary Magdalene was one of the most popular saints of the Middle Ages. The woman who had followed and served Jesus after he had cured her of all her illnesses (Luke 8:2) became the patron saint of many hospice chapels. The Crosiers thus saw her as a model of loving service. Medieval people also believed that she was the woman who anointed Jesus' feet (John 12:3). For the Crosiers, then, she became an example of hospitality. Finally, she had accompanied the Mother of God to the foot of the Cross of Christ and to his tomb (see Mark 15:40-47). Since Christ said, "whoever wishes to be my follower must deny himself, take up his cross each day, and follow in my footsteps" (Luke 9:23), the Crosiers considered Mary Magdalene a paragon of renunciation. Also the first to reach the tomb of Jesus after his resurrection, she recognized him when he called her by name "Mary," and responded, "Teacher!" before rushing off to tell the disciples that she had seen the Risen Christ (see John 20:11-18). The Crosiers thus saw her as an example of gratitude and joy.

[10]On the feast of Mary Magdalene the Crosiers sang to her the hymn *Laus tibi Christe*. See the *Hymnarium Sanctae Agathae,* 163-167.

9

The Order's Modern Revival:
1840 to the Present

On November 28, 1840, King William II of the Netherlands (1840–1849) promulgated a decree which allowed those monasteries which still existed in his kingdom to admit new members. By this time, as we have already seen, only two Crosier monasteries still existed, both in the Netherlands, that of St. Agatha near Cuijk and that in Uden. In these two monasteries were only four Crosiers, three at St. Agatha and the other at Uden; the youngest was sixty-three.

Before William's accession, Catholics had been consistently discriminated against: they could not expect to hold a position in national government or city administration, and were hindered in the practice of their religion. The new king, however, was well-disposed toward Catholics; he intended to change all this and to allow his Catholic subjects to participate fully in national life.

New members sought admission to the Crosier Order that same year. Some were young students, but there were also a number of diocesan priests, men who had wanted to enter the Order in their youth but had been kept from doing so by law. One such was Henricus Van Den Wijmelenberg, whom Pope Gregory XVI appointed the Order's administrator general in 1841. (Because it had been impossible to convoke a general chapter or elect a prior general, an administrator general had governed what was left of the Order since 1806.)[1]

---

[1] See Jan Scheerder, O.S.C., "De Kruisheren van Sint-Agatha en Uden in de jaren 1800–1840," *Clairlieu* 31 (1973) 3–54.

The number of new members increased so rapidly that the administrator general soon decided that another monastery should be founded. Still fearing interference from the Dutch government, Van Den Wijmelenberg chose to locate the new monastery in Belgium, where he believed the Order had better prospects for the future. He felt quite strongly about this, and even thought that a Belgian foundation was essential to the Order's survival.

In 1845 the Crosiers were welcomed to the Belgian city of Diest, where they were able to purchase the old church of St. Barbara and its adjoining buildings. Seven years later, the citizens of the city asked the Crosiers to establish an elementary and secondary school, which they did, despite the opposition of a liberal city administration.[2]

The new foundation in Diest brought great joy and enthusiasm to the members of the rejuvenated Order, and they soon began to look elsewhere for opportunities to expand further. In 1848 two Crosiers went to the islands of Curaçao and Saba in the West Indies, and two others to Wisconsin in the United States, but neither effort managed to gain a foothold or achieve anything permanent for the Order.[3]

After a revision of their national constitution in 1848, Dutch Catholics petitioned Pope Pius IX to re-establish their country's ecclesiastical hierarchy, which had been in abeyance for three centuries. The Pope granted their request in 1853. That same year, the Order's membership had risen to forty-six. Van Den Wijmelenberg determined that it was time for the Crosiers to normalize their administration once more, too, and convoked a general chapter, the first since 1784.[4]

[2]See W. Sangers, O.S.C., and G. Van Der Linden, *De Kruisheren te Diest 1845-1945* (Diest, 1945).

[3]See A. De Smet, *La communauté belge du nord-est du Wisconsin, ses origines, son évolution jusque vers 1900* (Wavre, 1957); J. Rausch, O.S.C., *The Crosier Story: A History of the Crosier Fathers in the United States* (Onamia, MN, 1960), 31-90; W. Sangers, O.S.C., *Father Eduard Daems, O.S.C., 1826-1879, de vader van de kolonisten in Wisconsin,* Xaveriana (Louvain, 1939); A. Van Asseldonk, O.S.C., "De ouders van Franciscus Daems," *Clairlieu* 11 (1953) 42-44. See also *Clairlieu* 14 (1956) 92.

[4]See J. Scheerder, O.S.C., *Henricus van den Wijmelenberg; een religieuse emancipator in Oost-Brabant 1800-1881. De nieuwe lente in de orde van het H. Kruis,* Bijdragen tot de geschiedenis van het zuiden van Nederland (Tilburg, 1976); and "Acta Capitulorum Generalium 1840-1940," *Chronicon Cruciferorum. Synopsis Memorabil-*

That Chapter elected Van Den Wijmelenberg their master general, the title modern Crosiers use for the head of the Order. The chapter also restored the post of definitor, or general councilor, and elected the traditional four members to this office. Besides these elections, the chapter made two important decisions which needed and received papal approval: first, in the future the property and income of each monastery would belong to the Order; second, henceforth the master general would have the power to transfer any Crosier.

In 1855 Simon Gielen, the prior of St. Agatha, died. He had held his office since 1805, and had succeeded in preserving his monastery and its way of life during one of the most difficult periods of the Order's history. On Gielen's death, the master general, who had lived in Uden since 1840 and was the local superior there, moved to St. Agatha and became its prior.

Thus the Crosier Order began its revival.

An order's vitality in large measure derives from how it builds its life and work upon the tradition and spirituality which it has inherited from the past. As master general, Van Den Wijmelenberg was faced with the enormous task of first recovering the tradition, the spirituality, and the work of the Crosiers in times past, and then encouraging his confreres to adopt this way of life for the contemporary Order. To help achieve the first of these goals, he engaged the historian C. R. Hermans to investigate the Order's documents, which had been widely scattered when its monasteries were suppressed. By 1858 Hermans had gathered a large number of these sources and was able to publish them in a three-volume collection,[5] which continues to be an indispensable manual for anyone studying the history of the Crosiers.

Naturally we must ask if the Order found in these documents from its past the guidance and inspiration which it needed for the present.

The master general certainly did. Until his death Van Den Wijmelenberg endeavored to persuade the members of his Order to be good Crosiers in the tradition of their community. He always stressed

ium Sacri et Canonici Ordinis Sanctae Crucis 1, fasc. 2:112–116, fasc. 3:266–278, fasc. 4:389–402; 2, fasc. 2:146–160; 3, fasc. 1:81–210.

[5]*Annales Canonicorum Regularium S. Augustini Ordinis Sanctae Crucis* ('s Hertoogenbosch, 1858) with *Index* (Diest, 1953). See T. J. Van De Ven, "Dr. C. R. Hermans, Leven en werk van de pionier van de Noordbrabantse geschiedschrijving in de 19e eeuw," *Brabantia* 7 (1958) 183–206, 211–234.

that the Crosiers were canons regular and thus obliged to choral prayer of the Divine Office and the daily celebration of community Mass together. Consequently, he always worked for an Order-wide uniformity in choral prayer and liturgy. But he did more. Although the Crosiers belong to the family of canons regular, they have also been distinguished by their special devotion to the Cross throughout the centuries. They have seen their red-and-white cross not only as a symbol of Christ's victory but of his love, which they chose to manifest above all by their care for the needy. Van Den Wijmelenberg encouraged the Order's traditional veneration of the Cross, and when the Roman Congregation of Rites compelled the Crosiers to adopt the Roman Breviary and Missal in 1856, he persuaded the Congregation to allow the Order to retain a number of its own special celebrations, most notably the seven "Passion liturgies" during Lent.

During the seventeenth and eighteenth centuries the Crosiers had steadily increased their involvement in the education of young people, frequently admitting to their schools, as a form of service to the needy, students whose parents could not pay the necessary fees. After 1840 the Crosiers returned to this work in Uden and Diest, and in 1855 were asked to return to Maaseik (Belgium) on condition that they found an elementary and secondary school.[6] There, too, they provided students from less affluent families the opportunity for a better education.

During the last years of his administration, Van Den Wijmelenberg was greatly pained by a lawsuit which the Dutch government brought against the monastery of St. Agatha. Although the government had confiscated the monastery's property in the sixteenth century, the Crosiers had been allowed, on payment of an annual fee, to continue managing the estate and to keep the income it produced. In the nineteenth century, however, the government sued the Crosiers for both management and income. The Crosiers lost the suit, and in 1889 this remnant of the monastery's former possessions was transferred to the Dutch government. The financial loss to the monastery of St. Agatha and to the Order as a whole was very serious.

---

[6] *De Kruisheren te Maaseik,* 215–329. Around this same time the Crosiers also tried to return to their former church and monastery at Venlo; see J. Scheerder, O.S.C., "De onderhandelingen over de terugkeer van de Kruisheren te Venlo," *Clairlieu* 34 (1976) 11–64.

Henricus Van Den Wijmelenberg died on March 25, 1881. The Crosiers honor him as the second founder of their Order.

The two men who succeeded Van Den Wijmelenberg as master general, Wilhelmus Smits (1881-1889) and Martinus Manders (1889-1899) had both been prior of the Uden monastery before their elections and continued to live there afterwards, holding both offices simultaneously. During their terms, the Crosiers showed no great spirit of enterprise and found themselves faced with additional setbacks. Financial difficulties forced the Crosiers of Diest to close their school in 1885, although the next year the community at Uden founded a secondary school for young men interested in the priesthood.[7] In 1887 the Order attempted to return to England after a three-century absence, but failed. Despite the difficulties, the Crosiers worked hard at preserving and improving their religious life. By 1899 the Order numbered ninety-one members and had four monasteries, two in the Netherlands and two in Belgium.

That same year Henricus Hollmann was elected master general.[8] Before his election, he had been prior of St. Agatha for eighteen years, where he continued to reside after becoming master general. Forty-six years old when elected, Hollmann was an enterprising man who would leave the Order much changed. Prior to 1900, the Crosiers' life and work had been confined to Belgium, France, England, the Netherlands, and the Rhineland and Westphalia in Germany. An additional limitation had been the strong feeling among its members that they were called to live and work in or near the monastery where they had first entered the Order. During Hollmann's term as master general (1899-1927), the Order truly became an international body as Crosiers established themselves all over the world. Although their numbers were still very limited, they showed an admirable enterprise and willingness to help people who needed help. Wherever they went, their confreres at home continued to show an interest in how they lived and in what they did.

The next three decades greatly widened the Order's horizons. In 1903 the Crosiers returned to Wallonia, the French-speaking part of Belgium, with the building of a monastery, a church, and a school

---

[7]See J. Scheerder, O.S.C., *Prior A. G. van Mil* (Diest, 1967), and L. Heere, O.S.C., "Studenten der Latijnse- en Hoogschool van Uden," *Clairlieu* 6 (1948) 53-65.

[8]See J. Scheerder, O.S.C., "Henricus Martinus Franciscus Hollmann, 52ste Magister Generaal de Orde van het H. Kruis, 1853-1927," *Clairlieu* 23-24 (1965-1966).

in Hannut. In 1910 there was a second attempt to establish the Order in the United States, when a group of Crosiers traveled to Minnesota in the company of pioneering settlers. These Crosiers at first worked among the settlers they had accompanied, but in 1922 they were able to build their first monastery and school in Onamia, Minnesota.[9] Feeling called to work on yet another continent, some Crosiers went to Africa in 1920. They had been given a huge mission territory, as large as the Netherlands and Belgium combined, in the north of what was then the Belgian Congo and is now Zaire.[10] Only seven years later, in 1927, the Crosiers were invited to care for a mission territory around the city of Bandung, Indonesia. In neither instance did the Crosiers shrink from the challenge; they were, in fact, happy to respond to such missionary opportunities.[11]

At home, too, the first decades of this century brought new Crosier foundations. In 1921 they began to operate a parish in Rotterdam in the Netherlands, and in 1926 were able to build a new monastery at Zoeterwoude, near Leiden, also in the Netherlands.[12] The monastery at Zoeterwoude was established as a school of philosophy for young Crosiers, since the monastery at St. Agatha, despite its enlargement in 1908, had become too small to house all the Order's students in the program of higher education leading to the priesthood. The Crosiers of Uden also had to build a new monastery and church, in 1904. In 1922 these Crosiers also began to build a new school, with facilities for boarding students. The new facilities were intended for young men who felt a call to the priesthood; when they finished their studies in Uden, they were completely free to enter any order or congregation they wished, or to continue on to the diocesan priesthood.

[9]See Rausch, *Crosier Story.*

[10]See L. Honhon, O.S.C., *De stichting der Kruisherenmissie in den Congo-Uele* (Diest, 1922).

[11]See G. Wester, O.S.C., "In de Gordel van Smaragd," *In Cruce Vita. De orde der Kruisheren in Nederland* (Rotterdam, 1936) 121–128; see also "Ordo salib suci di Indonesia," *Kami Yang Ditandi Salib Suci* (Bandung, 1977) 64–69.

[12]See H. Van Rooijen, O.S.C., "Het klooster in het polderland," *In Cruce Vita* (Rotterdam, 1936) 99–108; G. Wester, O.S.C., "In Rotterdam's groene gordel," *In Cruce Vita* (Rotterdam, 1936) 109–120; R. Schellekens, O.S.C., "Rotterdam, Herinneringen aan de stichting van klooster en parochie," *Chronicon Cruciferorum* 1, fasc. 3:231–256.

Since the Order had now become an international institution, the master general needed a representative in Rome. Accordingly, a procurator general was appointed in 1922, and the Crosiers have had a house in that city ever since.[13] The Crosiers were able to assume all these new responsibilities because their numbers were steadily growing. By 1930 the Order numbered 281 members, three times the ninety-one members it had had at the beginning of the century.

Like his predecessors, Master General Hollmann saw to it that his confreres conducted themselves as worthy members of their Order and that they faithfully recited the choral prayer required of good canons regular. He also promoted scholarship, and it is worth noting that many Crosiers published regularly during his generalate.[14]

During this period of growth, the Crosiers reflected more deeply on their specific character as members of an Order centered on the Cross of Christ. There was a growing desire to recover the devotion to the Cross which had characterized the Order's earlier centuries, and to find in that devotion the inspiration for a Crosier way of life. When the breviary was revised in 1914, the Order was deprived of its seven "Passion liturgies," but in 1923 the Congregation of Rites granted the Crosiers' request to reinstate these liturgies in the Order's calendar. Crosiers also continued to dedicate their new churches to the Holy Cross. Following an old tradition, several monasteries rang a bell at 3:00 p.m. to commemorate Christ's death on the Cross. When the Order drew up new Statutes in 1925, the following provision was added:

> Because a secondary goal of our Order is to foster devotion to the Cross and suffering of Christ among our members and among all people, so that all might grow in their love for our Savior, all our members shall meditate on the Cross and suffering of Christ and,

[13] The present Crosier monastery in Rome is attached to the seventh-century church of San Giorgio al Velabro in the heart of the ancient city; it is the residence of the Order's master general and its international headquarters.

[14] See D. Snijders, O.S.C., *Herman Linnebank 1875-1927. Zijn werk als criticus en Vlamingenvriend* (Antwerp, 1952); J. Scheerder, O.S.C., "Kruisheer L. G. J. Honhon, 1858-1942," *Clairlieu* 35 (1977) 3-88; A. Ramaekers, O.S.C., "Oudheidkundige, Dr. H. van Lieshout," *Het Oude Land van Loon* (1945) 1-7; and M. Brouns, O.S.C., "Henricus Petrus Paulus van Lieshout, leraar en schrijver," *Nationaal Biografisch Woordenboek* (Brussels, 1970) 4, cols. 508-512.

by their preaching and example, inspire others to venerate that Cross and suffering.

The next master general, William Van Dinter (1927–1940), further expanded the Order's international commitments by sending Crosiers to Belém do Para, Brazil, in 1934.[15] Van Dinter had thought of going to Brazil as a missionary himself in 1907, but because there had been no possibility of doing so, Hollmann had asked him to go to the United States in 1910, where he had later been appointed the first superior.

Even today older Crosiers still speak of Van Dinter's great love for the missions and for his missionary confreres. He sent most young Crosiers of his time to those missions, either to Java (Indonesia), to the Congo (Zaire), or to Brazil. Not every young Crosier set out enthusiastically, but the shortage of priests in the missions was great, and young priests could not always find an opportunity for priestly work in the Netherlands or Belgium.

Still, Van Dinter was able to build two more monasteries in the Netherlands: at Neeritter in the province of Limburg and at Nijmegen (1937). The former became the novitiate house, the latter a center for the missions. Since 1932, a Crosier has served a small parish at Odiliapeel. In Belgium, too, the Crosiers were able to make one more foundation, at Achel, where their seminarians received their philosophical education before moving to Diest for theology.

When Van Dinter died in September 1940, it was impossible to hold the election of a new master general because of World War II. Vicars general thus governed the Order until 1946.

At the general chapter convoked in 1946, Wilhelmus Van Hees, prior of the monastery at Uden, was elected the new master general and has held the post until the present.[16] During the first ten years of his term, he lived at St. Agatha, as his immediate predecessors had done, but later moved the Order's generalate to Amersfoort, the Netherlands.

---

[15]See H. Plag, O.S.C., " 'Iter Para tutum.' Bij het vijfde lustrum van de Kruisheren in Brazilië," *Chronicon Cruciferorum* 2, fasc. 3:221–254.

[16]Editor's note: Master General Van Hees died in December 1981 and was succeeded the following February by Lambert Graus, O.S.C., who had been provincial of the Belgian Crosiers.

That same year, 1956, the Order was divided into three provinces: the province of St. Augustine (the Netherlands and Germany); the province of Blessed Theodore de Celles (Belgium); and the province of St. Odilia (the United States). A fourth province, that of Bom Jesus (Brazil), was added in 1967 and a fifth, that of Sang Kristus (Java, Indonesia), was established in 1977.

This division was made necessary by the Order's continued growth. The number of monasteries had doubled, and the Crosiers were active in many new locations. In 1953 Cardinal Frings, archbishop of Cologne, enabled the Crosiers to return to Germany. They came back to Wuppertal-Elberfeld and to their former monastery in Ehrenstein near Neustadt-on-the-Wied. Today the Crosiers in Germany serve eleven parishes: St. Suitbertus and St. Laurentius in Wuppertal-Elberfeld; St. Hedwig in Wuppertal-Hahnerberg; St. Mary Magdalene in Wuppertal-Beyenburg, where they re-occupied an old Crosier monastery; Holy Cross and St. Gall in Bonn; St. Christopher in Breitscheid; St. John Vianney in Lintorf; St. Joseph in Kettwig Vor Der Brücke; Holy Trinity in Ehrenstein; and Christ the King in Essen-Haarzopf.

Because the American Crosiers wanted a mission project of their own, they were entrusted with a mission territory in Dutch New Guinea in 1958. This later became the the diocese of Agats-Asmat in Irian Jaya, Indonesia.

In 1967 a group of Belgian Crosiers settled in the Leopoldau district of Vienna, Austria, where they assumed the care of a very large parish containing twenty-five thousand people.

There have been setbacks during these years, too.

In 1962 the Congregation of Rites, after another examination of the feasts proper to the Order, removed the "Passion liturgies" from the Order's calendar once again. As a kind of compensation, however, the Crosiers have been allowed since 1960 to celebrate the Liturgy of the Hours and the Mass of the Holy Cross on each Friday throughout the year, provided that no feast is assigned to that day. In practice, meditation and preaching on the Cross has been left to each Crosier's personal discretion, and it is not yet possible to judge whether veneration of the Cross is diminishing among some of the Order's members.

The Crosiers have also lost many of their members. In 1965, twenty-four Crosier missionaries were murdered in Zaire.[17] This has not, however, discouraged the Belgian Crosiers from continuing their good and admirable work in that country. And, as has been the case with many orders, a number of Crosiers have left the Order in the course of the last ten years.

Today the Crosier Order numbers 619 members worldwide.[18] Considering the broad field in which the Crosiers work, this number is too small. There are new recruits in the United States, Indonesia, and Brazil, but very few in Europe. We ask our readers to join the Crosiers in praying to God to call young men to carry on the ideals of the Crosiers today as others have done in the past.

[17]See A. Lantin, O.S.C., *Gedenkboek voor vierentwintig bloedgetuigen van de Kruisheren-orde in de missielanden Kongo en Irian Barat* (Diest, 1966); J. Verhoeven, O.S.C., *Gijzelaars onder Makondo* (Diest, 1965); and L. Raedschelders, O.S.C., ed., *Buta 1965* (Opglabbeek, Belgium: Paesen, 1990).

[18]Editor's note: Such was the case when Father Van Den Bosch completed this history in 1978. Since then, additional departures and deaths have caused the Order's membership to decline significantly: the statistics released for the General Chapter of 1991 show a membership of 467 men and a rising median age.

Appendix

The Crosiers in the United States and Indonesia

This appendix has been added to Father Van Den Bosch's history of the Crosier Order in order to make the book a more complete reference for readers outside of northern Europe. In it we will summarize the story of the Crosiers in the United States after their second attempt to establish a North American foundation[1] and of the Crosiers who settled in the diocese of Bandung, Indonesia, in 1927.

The Crosier monastery and seminary at Onamia, Minnesota; the motherhouse of the American Crosiers, established in 1922.

[1]For the story of the first Crosier settlement in the United States, in Wisconsin during the middle of the nineteenth century, see Rausch, *Crosier Story,* 31-90.

131

Although the enterprising Master General Hollmann must have cast longing eyes on the great potential offered by the land across the Atlantic, the immediate occasion for sending some Crosiers was a request for Dutch-speaking priests to accompany new settlers who were being encouraged to emigrate to the United States by land developers and by priests who hoped to increase the Catholic presence in the new land. The first three Crosiers, led by Fr. William Van Dinter, arrived in Butler, Minnesota, with a group of Dutch settlers in March, 1910. Five more Crosiers arrived the following October, enabling the little group of pioneers to establish a second parish at Onamia. The parish at Butler, which the Crosiers continued to serve until 1970, never became more than a country parish; Onamia, however, proved to be the place where the Crosier presence in the United States truly took root.

The first residence in Onamia was merely the local parish rectory. It served as an informal center of community for the seven priests and four brothers who arrived in the United States before the outbreak of World War I and who lived alone or in pairs in various parishes. (This type of parish work continues to play an important

The golden jubilee celebration held at Onamia in 1960 in commemoration of the Crosiers' arrival in the U.S. and the Order's 750th anniversary of foundation.

part in the work of the Onamia Crosiers.) After the war, Master General Hollmann, accompanied by three more priests and one brother, visited the United States. At his insistence a monastery was constructed in Onamia in 1922, and on September 14 of that year a formal house was established and a prior elected. At the same time seven students were admitted to the new school, and Crosier Seminary was born.

Since its beginnings Onamia has maintained its important place in American Crosier life. The physical plant was expanded in 1925, 1939, 1950, and 1957. By the early 1960s the school numbered about three hundred students, but declining vocations thereafter reduced the number by two-thirds two decades later. The high cost of education, a reduced number of Crosiers to serve as faculty and staff and a smaller number of young men from which to recruit led to the decision, in 1989, to close the school. The monastery continues, however, and provides a variety of services to the American Crosier province, to the local community and to parishes in the area. In 1991 the school building was leased to Nexus, a residential center which provides an intensive therapeutic program for young men between the ages of thirteen and eighteen.

The Crosier monastery and retreat-renewal center in Hastings, Nebraska.

As students graduated from the seminary program at Onamia and sought admission to the Order, the need for more space was keenly felt. This led to the purchase of a former academy for girls in Hastings, Nebraska, which was opened as the Crosier novitiate and major seminary in the fall of 1932, and became a formal house in 1936. In 1952 the school of philosophy was moved to Fort Wayne, Indiana, and followed by the school of theology in 1955. A large addition was built onto the original building in Hastings in 1962 to house the novitiate and formation program for brothers. Declining vocations in recent years led the Hastings Crosiers to decide to open a retreat center in the unused portions of the monastery, which also supplied personnel and space for the activities of the province's mission office. Further changes in the role of the Hastings community came in 1988, when the novitiate was transferred, and in 1990, when the monastery was designated as the residence site for those older Crosiers who need supervisory care.

The success of the seminary at Onamia was encouraging and, as the number of American Crosiers grew, a similar program was established in Fort Wayne, Indiana. In 1938 another building which had been an academy for girls was purchased and, after a year of remodeling, was opened as a seminary in 1939. This venture also proved successful and, a few years later, plans were made for a new building. The carrying out of these plans was prevented by the outbreak of World War II.

Master General William Van Hees, O.S.C., with the staff and student body of the Crosier major seminary at Fort Wayne, Indiana, in 1960.

After the war, the Crosiers' plans changed. In 1948 the Fort Wayne community moved to Wawasee, Indiana, to staff a seminary owned by the diocese of Fort Wayne. The building in Fort Wayne was then transformed into the school of philosophy and theology for young Crosiers. As their number increased, the decision was made to build a completely new plant. This was done in two stages, in 1955 and 1963–1964. For many years Fort Wayne also served as the residence of the Order's vicar general in the United States and later its provincial superior. A high point in its history was the hosting of the Crosiers' 1973 general chapter. Shortly afterwards the theology program was transferred to Catholic Theological Union in Chicago and the residence for those in the undergraduate program to St. Peter's Parish in St. Cloud, Minnesota. (The Crosiers also assumed the care of the parish soon afterwards.) The Fort Wayne monastery was then adapted for retreats and other programs until 1983. The community was officially terminated in 1985.

The Wawasee Crosiers purchased the building which housed their minor seminary from the diocese in 1964. Shortly afterwards, as seminary vocations declined, the school was gradually transformed into a boarding school dedicated to imparting Christian principles of living to students from a broad variety of backgrounds. Financial difficulties and the strain of harmonizing religious life with the demands of the school's new program led to the closing of both school and monastery in 1975.

In 1954 Crosiers were sent to White Plains, New York, to serve as faculty members of Archbishop Stepinac High School along with priests of the archdiocese of New York and members of other religious communities. In 1957 the Crosiers acquired a residence in White Plains and erected a priory. As the proportion of Crosiers working in the archdiocesan high school diminished, the community moved out of the house, which was owned by the archdiocese, and purchased its own residence in New Rochelle. Today most members of this community serve as chaplains to religious communities and to other groups in the area.

Shortly after the erection of a Crosier province in the United States in 1957, thoughts turned to establishing a mission area where its members could work. Led by Fr. Frank Pitka, O.S.C., the first three American Crosier foreign missionaries arrived in Agats, then part of Dutch New Guinea, at the end of 1958. This mission has enjoyed the enthusiastic support of the American Crosiers throughout its history. As the number of Catholics in the mission area grew, a new diocese was created in 1969, with Alphonse Sowada, O.S.C., as its first bishop. The first novice from the area entered the Order in 1978 and was ordained a priest in 1983. One of the less happy experiences of the mission was the death of Fr. Jan Smit, O.S.C., who was shot to death by an official of the Indonesian government in 1965.

In 1960 the Crosiers founded a new parish in Shoreview, Minnesota, under the patronage of St. Odilia. Over the years it has grown into a very large and active parish, with an elementary school. The parish rectory also serves as a monastery for Crosiers working in the parish and elsewhere in the area. In 1988 the Shoreview community became the province's house of novitiate.

In 1972 several Crosiers who wished to live a more traditional form of Crosier religious life established a house at Rocky Ridge, Maryland. Shortly afterwards a more suitable residence, formerly a house of novitiate for sisters, was found in nearby Beallsville. The members of this community are involved in teaching at Mount St. Mary's Seminary at Emmitsburg, research for church planning, neighboring parishes, and retreats for individuals and small groups.

A common residence was established for several Crosiers working in parishes in southern Michigan at the parish rectory in Three Rivers in 1975. This small community subsequently moved to the rectory of St. Joseph's Parish in Kalamazoo. Until the community's demise in 1989, these Crosiers were involved in teaching and in working at the diocesan chancery in addition to their work in the parish. The Crosiers were also invited into another diocese in Michigan, that of Detroit, in 1976. A community was established with its center at the rectory of St. Cyprian's Parish in the Detroit suburb of Riverview.

Following the general trend of establishing consortia of theological schools in which several religious orders participate, the Crosiers joined the Catholic Theological Union in Chicago in 1976. During their first two years in Chicago, they rented their residence. In 1978 a house was purchased to serve as a home for Crosier students and their directors and for several other Crosiers working in various apostolates in the Chicago area.

In 1978 a separate house for the provincial and his staff was established in St. Paul, Minnesota. At first it served as both a residence and the location of the provincial offices. In 1984 separate office space was rented from the parish of St. Helena in Minneapolis. The provincial offices coordinate the many activities of the province and those connected with the mission in Agats.

In 1979 the Crosiers assumed responsibility for St. Stephen's Parish in Anoka, Minnesota, another large parish in the archdiocese of St. Paul. The rectory serves as a monastery for the parish staff as well as for other Crosiers working in the Minneapolis–St. Paul area.

As members of the province grew older and began to feel the rigors of northern climates more keenly, a monastery in a milder climate became more desirable. Some individual Crosiers had previously settled in Florida or Texas, but in 1983 the opportunity to establish a formal community in Phoenix, Arizona, presented itself. Although not all members of this community are of retirement age, those who are have found wholly new opportunities to continue their ministerial service. The large Spanish-speaking population of the area also offers an opportunity to those familiar with that language and culture to provide ministry to that part of the population.

Our account of the Crosiers in the United States has thus far avoided naming specific individuals. On the one hand, listing all those who could be mentioned would lengthen this appendix unduly; on the other, all American Crosiers deserve credit for their Order's success in this country. Nevertheless, we should take note of those men who have led the Crosiers in the United States since their arrival here.

William Van Dinter was the superior of the Crosiers who began arriving in 1910, and was elected the first prior of the monastery at Onamia in 1922. He also served as vicar general in the United States until he himself was elected master general in 1927. John Van Der Hulst succeeded Van Dinter as prior of Onamia and vicar general (1927–1933 and 1939–1942). Adrian Van Zutphen held the same positions between 1933 and 1939, and Lawrence Kerich between 1942 and 1948. During World War II, Rome appointed Fathers Van Der Hulst and Kerich administrators of the Crosier foundations in Brazil and Java as well. In 1947 Thomas Brandon, O.S.C., the first American to enter the Order, was appointed the Order's first full-time vicar general in the United States, a post he held until 1952, when Father Kerich succeeded him.

When the American Crosier province was established in 1957, Benno Mischke, O.S.C., was elected its first provincial and served until 1969. He was succeeded by Richard John, O.S.C. (1969–1978) and Daniel Davidson, O.S.C. (1978–1986). The present provincial is Fr. Robert Rossi, O.S.C.

In 1990 the Crosiers celebrated the 780th anniversary of the foundation of their Order and the eightieth anniversary of their second arrival in the United States. At that time the province had about 115 members in the United States and a dozen more in the mission region of Agats.

Less than twenty years after the Crosiers arrived in the United States, the Congregation for the Propagation of the Faith, through the good offices of Cardinal Van Rossum, offered the Order a role in the mission to the island of Java, Indonesia. Although the Crosiers had accepted a mission in the Congo (Zaire) only a few years before, they had the courage to respond to this new offer as well, for experience had shown them that missionary effort would attract vocations to the Order and thus assure a solid future.

So it was that three Crosiers arrived in Bandung on February 9, 1927. These were Marinus Nillesen, O.S.C., Jan De Rooij, O.S.C., and Jacobus Goumans, O.S.C., who was later appointed apostolic vicar and, in 1942, ordained bishop. Since there were very few Indonesian and Chinese Catholics at the time, the Crosiers continued the work of their Jesuit predecessors: the pastoral care of the Dutch

The Crosier major seminarians of the Province of Sang Kristus, Indonesia, with their provincial superior, Fr. Yan Sunyata, O.S.C., in 1988.

and Indian-European population. The work of the mission was confined to Bandung, Ceribon, and Cimahi (a Dutch garrison town), although the Crosiers did visit Catholics on the nearby tea and sugar plantations with some regularity. Since not all those who would be sent as missionaries to Bandung had finished their studies, some Crosiers were temporarily borrowed from the Crosiers in the United States. When young Crosier missionaries regularly began arriving from the Netherlands, the mission work intensified.

This allowed the Crosiers to turn their attention to the native Indonesian population in earnest, for which they chose to center their efforts in Cicadas, on the east side of Bandung. Nor was the Chinese part of the population overlooked: these people were served by a center, including a church and a school, on Waringin-Kebon Jati Street on the west side of the city and at Melania, a settlement which included schools and a clinic, on the north side of the city. Meanwhile, contacts were also being established with people outside Bandung. As a sign of appreciation for the missionary zeal of the Crosiers, their region was raised to the status of an apostolic prefecture in 1932, and to that of an apostolic vicariate in 1941.

The Crosier novices of the Province of Sang Kristus, Indonesia, with Master General Lambert Graus, O.S.C., and their provincial superior, Fr. Yan Sunyata, O.S.C., in 1988.

Progress more or less came to a halt during the Japanese occupation of Java (1942–1945). Priests were interned, and the whole vicariate was left to the care of the one priest who remained free. After the war there was a great shortage of missionaries; many had died in the internment camps and others had returned to the Netherlands because of poor health. Fortunately, the Dutch Crosiers were able to send a number of young men to Indonesia. Because many Europeans were then leaving Indonesia, the missionaries were able to give their attention almost entirely to the Indonesian people. Their work was blessed, and the churches remained full in spite of the departure of the Dutch and other Europeans. A very important event was the formation of the Catholic University of Parahyangan in 1955.

Up to this point, however, Catholic Indonesians were mainly people of Middle Javanese origin. Hardly any Catholics were to be found among the local Sundanese people of West Java, the ethnic group which made up most of the population of the diocese of Bandung. Contact with the Sundanese did not really begin until 1964, when the govenment disbanded a religious group called Jawa-Sunda Religion (abbreviated as ADS in Indonesian). Soon after, the leaders of ADS began to join the Catholic Church because its doctrines, especially those about love for others and marriage, were not far from their own ideals. A pronouncement by the founder of ADS may also have had a significant impact: "Afterwards seek your shelter under a white fir tree which can bring peace and salvation to the world." He explained this statement as a reference to the doctrines of the New Testament, the teaching of Christ, and especially the teaching of Christian love. Thousands of their followers emulated the example of the ADS leadership.

The massive influx of former members of ADS opened a new field of mission work and challenged the missionaries to develop new approaches. Since the reasons for which former members of ADS were becoming Catholic were not always that clear, there was a need for intensive catechesis. Because these catechumens usually lived in remote areas difficult to reach, special teams were formed and commissioned to carry out the instruction. The great majority of former members of ADS were baptized and given additional care by pastors and catechists from Middle Java and the Sundanese area who had received their training at the Catechetical Higher School in Jogjakarta.

The missionaries also worked to improve the standard of living of their new converts. The results of these efforts became obvious within ten to twelve years with the growing number of Catholic religious organizations and credit unions and the establishment of the Sulanjana Foundation, which promotes improvements in agriculture and husbandry. Many young people continued their studies in institutions of higher education, in nursing schools, and in the minor seminary. There were even a number of young men, former members of ADS, who pursued courses in philosophy and theology at the major seminary of Suryagung Bumi in Bandung, and today there are a number of Sundanese priests. The missionaries have not overlooked the introduction of elements of Sundanese culture into liturgy and other ceremonies, either: the Sundanese language is used in prayer, preaching, and liturgical singing accompanied by indigenous musical instruments.

Although the Crosiers came to Indonesia as missionaries, they did not forget that they were also religious, members of the Order of the Holy Cross. Only three in number at first and heavily burdened by pastoral work, they clung to their ideal: an apostolate arising from community life. Work was adjusted to meet the demands of community life: meals, recreation, and prayer in common, discussions about the apostolate, and recollection days.

After only two or three years of missionary work by the Crosiers, some young men felt called to this way of life. At first, these candidates were sent either to the Netherlands or to Middle Java to be educated for the priesthood, but as the Crosiers in Indonesia began to reorganize their missionary work after the paralyzing disruption of World War II, they adopted important changes in their formation program. The Indonesian struggle for independence caused concern that Western missionaries might not be admitted to the country any longer, so a minor seminary was opened at Cicadas. An additional consideration in opening this school was that it enabled the local people to see with their own eyes that candidates for the priesthood were actually being trained among them. The Crosiers hoped that this would encourage other young men to more readily consider a vocation to the priesthood and, in fact, students from Bandung and the surrounding towns did begin to enter the minor seminary.

The next step was to open a major seminary in Cicadas, which had to be staffed by the already heavily-burdened priests from the parishes. This program was open to all young men interested in the priesthood, but when the student finished his studies in philosophy, he was expected to choose between being becoming a diocesan priest or a Crosier. There were only three students at first, but the number grew, and eventually the seminary was moved to the rectory on Pandu Street. When the decision was made to open a Crosier novitiate there as well, the rectory became the first monastery of the Indonesian Crosiers in 1957. The Crosier program of major seminary studies was later added to this novitiate. Candidates for the brotherhood also began to apply, but only one of them remained with the Order.

As political circumstances made contact with the Crosier Province of St. Augustine in the Netherlands more difficult, a proprovince was established in Bandung in 1962. Although a first step toward greater independence, the proprovince continued to depend on the Province of St. Augustine for financial help and personnel.

In 1967 the Crosier major seminary in Bandung was expanded to admit priesthood candidates from Bogor, Bangka, Lampung (on the island of Sumatra), Sintang, and Ketapang (on the island of Kalimantan), as well as a few military catechists and some Ursuline and Dominican sisters. Its name was changed from the Scholasticate of the Crosier Order to the Institute for Philosophy and Theology (abbreviated as IFT in Indonesian). Since space in the the Pandu monastery could no longer meet the needs of the IFT, a new building was erected, with outside financial help, on Nias Street in the middle of Bandung. To further meet the new requirements, the pastorteachers were replaced with qualified personnel. When the IFT received government accreditation, its name was changed again, to the Higher School of Philosophy and Theology (abbreviated as STFT in Indonesian). Further government regulations obliged the STFT to associate itself with a university, so in 1983 it became a department of the Catholic University of Parahyangan in Bandung and was designated as the university's faculty of philosophy.

Additional personnel from the Netherlands can no longer be counted on, but fortunately the number of Indonesian Crosier *fraters* (members of the Order who have taken their vows and are studying for the priesthood) is quite satisfactory. When the monastery on Pandu Street became too small to house the Order's novices and students, the Crosiers purchased the monastery of the Brothers of St. Aloysius to use as a novitiate when the Brothers left Bandung in 1975.

This growth was evidence that the proprovince would soon be able to stand on its own. Consequently, on July 20, 1977, the Crosiers celebrated fifty years of living and working in the mission of Indonesia with the crowning of their work: the formal erection of the Crosier Province of Sang Kristus.[2]

This progress made it necessary to give thought to the future, especially to the formation of these young Crosiers to educate the next generation. Consequently, some of them were sent to Louvain, Rome, and Manila for higher studies. A few priests and fraters were also put at the disposal of Bishop Sowada, the American Crosier bishop in Agats, each to serve a few years.

Over time, there has been a growing sense of a need to give greater attention to the Crosiers' own specific spirituality. With the support of the late Bishop Peter Arntz of Bandung, the Crosiers took the initiative of establishing a center for spiritual formation for both its own membership and the diocese. Before these plans could be realized, however, Bishop Arntz died suddenly on April 25, 1984. A few months later a diocesan priest, Alexander Djajasiswaja, who had been vicar general of the diocese of Semarang, was named the new bishop of Bandung and ordained to that office in November, 1984; he is the first non-Crosier to assume pastoral care of the diocese of Bandung. The Crosiers now face the new challenge of defining their own identity independently of the diocese.[3]

---

[2]A clearer idea of the rapid growth of the Order's Indonesian province in recent years can be gained from some statistical data. In 1979, the province had thirty European and fourteen native Indonesian priests. By 1985, there were twenty-six native Indonesian and twenty-three European Crosier priests. Statistics prepared for the Order's 1991 General Chapter show that the province has ninety-nine members, most of whom are native Indonesians, with a median age of thirty-seven. Of these Crosiers, approximately sixty are in formation for the priesthood.

[3]This account of the Crosiers in Indonesia was summarized from *Kami Yang Ditandi Salib Suci* (Bandung, 1977) with some additions.

Bibliography

Acta Capitulorum Generalium 1840–1940. *Cronicon Cruciferorum.* *Synopsis Memorabilium Sacri et Canonici Ordinis Sanctae Crucis* 1, fasc. 2:112–116, fasc. 3:266–278, fasc. 4:389–402; 2, fasc. 2:146–160; 3, fasc. 1:81–210. Unpublished material circulated in dittographed and mimeographed form.

Aretz, H. "Das Kreuzherrenkloster Hohenbusch." *Rheinesche Post* (1976–1977).

Auvray, L. *Les régistres de Gregoire IX.* Paris, 1896.

Bau- und Kunstdenkmäler von Westfalen. Münster: Kreis Brilon, 1952.

Beck, E. "The Order of the Holy Cross in England." *Transactions of the Royal Historical Society* 3rd series 7 (1913) 191–208.

Berlière, O.S.B., U. "Les Croisiers de Namur." *Monasticon Belge* 1:150–152, 189–190, 462, 490. Maredsous, 1890–1897.

————. "Monastère des Croisiers à Dinant." *Monasticon Belge* 1:148–150, 188–189. Maredsous, 1890–1897.

————. "Monastère des Croisiers à Tournai." *Monasticon Belge* 1:460–463, 488. Maredsous, 1890–1897.

Bohr, F. *Aus dem alten Dülken.* Viersen, 1976.

Bovesse, J. "Les Croisiers de Namur." *Inventaire général sommaire des archives ecclésiastiques de la province de Namur.* Brussels, 1962.

Brandts, R. *Inventar des Archivs der Pfarrkirche St. Antonius in Wickrath.* Landschaftsverband Rheinland, Inventare nichtstaatlicher Archive 4. Düsseldorf, 1957.

Brouns, O.S.C., M. "Henricus Petrus Paulus van Lieshout, leraar en schrijver." *Nationaal Biografisch Woordenboek* 4, cols. 508-512. Brussels, 1970.

Brouwers, D. D. "Privilèges au Croisiers par le magistrat de Dinant en 1491." *Namurcum* 12 (1935) 17-21.

Buchet, A. *Le prieuré des Croisiers de Brandenbourg à Raeren, 1477-1784.* Verviers, 1948.

Büld, H. *Rheine an den Ems, Chroniken und Augenzeugenberichte, 1440-1950.* Rheine, 1977.

Bulloch, J. "The Crutched Friars." *Records of the Scottish Church History Society* 10 (1949) 89-106.

Büttner, R. *Die Säkularisation der Kölner geistlichen Institutionen.* Cologne, 1971.

Candels, H. *Das Prämonstratenserinnenstift Wenau.* Mönchengladbach, 1974.

Chettle, H. F. "The Friars of the Holy Cross in England." *History. The Journal of the Historical Association* 34 (1949) 204-220.

Clairlieu. *Tijdschrift gewijd aan de geschiedenis der Kruisheren.* Kruisherenklooster, 3581 Achel, Belgium.

Close, C. *Dinant. Notes d'histoire et de folklore.* Brussels, n.d.

Coenen, J. "De Pastoors van Heppeneert." *Miscellanea Gessleriana.* Antwerp, 1948.

Colson, O.S.C., M. "De eigendommem der Kruisheren van Maaseik en na de Franse Revolutie, 1797-1855." *Het Oude Land van Loon* 11 (1956) 121-160.

_____. "De Kruisheren van Venlo tijdens de Franse Revolutie." *Clairlieu* 13 (1956) 49-89 and 14 (1957) 3-59.

_____. *De rapporten van de Kantonkommissariseen, 1797-1800, Deel l'Maaseik.* Hasselt, 1969.

_____, and J. F. Gilmont. "La carrière mouvementée de Michel Mulot." *Musée Nauchâtelois* (1972) 245-255.

Corstens, S. "Die Anfänge des Kölner Buchdrucks." *Jahrb. d. Köln. Gesch. Vereins* 29-30 (1957) 1-97.

_____. "Die Blütezeit des Kölner Buchdrucks (15.-17. Jahrhundert)." *Rhein. Vierteljahrbl.* 40 (1976) 130-149.

Danhaive, F. "Le Croisiers de Namur." *Guetteur Wallon* 8 (1931) 3-36.

Deblon, A. "Les croisiers ordonnés à Liege aux 17ᵉ et 18ᵉ siècles." *Clairlieu* 33 (1975) 59-78.

De Gruyter, O.S.C., H., ed. *Constitutionum Hexapla*. Zouterwoude, 1951.

De Kruisheren te Maaseik, 1476-1797, 1855-1955. Diest, 1955.

Delaruelle, E. "Paix de Dieu et croissade dans le chretienté du XIIe siècle." *Cahiers de Fanjeux* 4 (1969) 27-60.

Depaire, J.-P. *La bibliothèque des Croisiers de Huy de Liège et de Namur*. 2 vols. Liege, 1969.

Dereine, Ch. "Chanoines." *Dictionnaire d'histoire et de géographie ecclésiastiques* 12:353-405. N.p., 1951.

De Ring, M. "Rodolphe de Zaeringen." *Messager des sciences historiques* (1841) 83-94.

De Smet, A. *La communauté belge du nord-est du Wisconsin, ses origines, son évolution jusque vers 1900*. Wavre, 1957.

Die Kunstdenkmäler der Rheinprovinz. Düsseldorf: Landkreis Trier, 1936.

Dohr, F. *Aus dem alten Dülken*. Viersen, 1976.

Domsta, H. J. "800 Jahre Schloss und Herrschaft Merode." *Einführung der Ausstellung im Schloss von Merode bei Düren*. N.p., 1974.

_____. *Geschichte der Fürsten von Merode im Mittelalter*. I. Band: Genealogie der Familie. Düren, 1974.

_____. "Schwarzenbroich. Zur Ausstattung des ehemaligen Kreuzherrenklosters." *Dürener Geschichtsblätter* 54 (1970) 1417-1448.

Douma, D. "Inventaris van het archief van het Kruisherenklooster Sint Agatha, 1371-1887." *Clairlieu* 28-29 (1970-1971).

_____. "De inventaris van het kloosterarchief van Sint Agatha en het belang ervan voor de geschiedenis van Oost-Brabant, Noord-Limburg en het Rijk van Nijmegen." *Het Land van Cuijk*. N.p., n.d.

_____. "Het klooster Sint Agatha en de Republiek der Verenigde Nederlanden, 1602-1794." *Merlet, driemaandelijks Blad, streekarchivariaat Land van Cuijk* 7 (1971) 118-132.

Drost, O.S.C., S. "Geschiedkundig overzicht van het Kruisherenklooster te Hoorn." *Geschiedk. Bladen* 2 (1906) 177-190.

Durand, A. "Le prieuré de Saint Ursin." *Clairlieu* 22 (1964) 53-90.

_____. "Le prieuré Sainte Croix de Caen." *Clairlieu* 25 (1967) 1-147.

Elm, K. "Entstehung und Reform des belgisch-nederländischen Kreuzherrenordens." *Zeitschrift für Kirchengeschichte* 82 (1971) 292-313.

Emmerich. 1200 Jahre Gymnasium. Emmerich, 1952.

Emond, O.S.C., L. "Het klooster Sint Agatha in de Lande van Cuijk." *Kruistriomf* 1-3 (1921-1924) *passim.*

———. *Kruisheren-missionarissen in de Nederlanden.* Cuijk: St. Agatha, 1933.

———. "De Maria-cultus in de Orde van het H. Kruis." *Ons Geestelijk Erf* 1 (1927) 49-55.

Evertz, G. *Kirchengeschichte der Pfarre Wegberg.* Wegberg, 1977.

———. "Pastor Sibenius, der Kreuzherr und religiöse Eiferer im und nach dem dreissigjährigen Krieg." *Clairlieu* 17 (1959) 18-25.

———. *Die Zeit der Französischen Fremdherrschaft, 1794-1814, in der Gemeinde Wegberg.* Wegberg, 1960.

Fackler, K. *Das alte Memmingen.* Memmingen, 1929.

Föhles, Th. *Aus längst vergangenen Tagen in Beyenburg.* Beyenburg, 1930.

Fontaine, O.S.C., E. "Les Croisiers de Liège en face de la suppression 1796." *Clairlieu* 7 (1949) 14-39.

———. "Le definitoire, 1796-1802." *Clairlieu* 10 (1952) 28-36.

———. "La fin de Clairlieu." *Clairlieu* 9 (1951) 6-42.

———. "Mgr. Jacques Dubois, Général des PP. Croisiers à Huy, 1778-1796." *Clairlieu* 4-5 (1946-1947) 1-223.

———. "Mgr. Jacques Dubois et la fin du prieuré de Carignan." *Clairlieu* 8 (1950) 49-66.

———. "Une première crise à Clairlieu au XVIIIe siècle, 1735-1752." *Clairlieu* 8 (1950) 3-30.

Francino, O.S.C., J. *Geschiedenis van de Orde der Kruisheren.* Utrecht, 1948.

———. "Onder Maria's bescherming." *In Cruce Vita. De orde der Kruisheren in Nederland.* Rotterdam, 1936.

Frenken, A. M. "De latere kerkvisitaties." *Bossche Bijdragen* 27 (1963-1964) 20-29.

Führer durch die Geschichte und die Kunstwerke der Heilig-Kreuz-Kirche in Aachen. Aachen, 1977.

Führer, A. *Geistliche Nachrichten über Medebach und seine Nachbarorte.* Naumburg, 1938.

———. "Die Pächter des Klosters Glindfeld in den Jahren 1500-1700." *Sauerländer Zeitung,* special edition (1932-1933).

Funken, J. "Das Kreuzherrenkloster in Venlo als Grundeigentümer in Leuth." *Heimatbuch des Grenzkreises Kempen-Krefeld.* 1962.

Gaier-Lhoest, J. *L'évolution topographique de la ville Dinant au moyen âge*. Brussels, 1964.

Galliot, C. F. J. *Histoire général ecclésiastique et civile de la ville et province de Namur*. 3 vols. Liege, 1788.

Gatzweiler, O. *Die liturgischen Handschriften des Aachener Münsterstifts*. Münster, 1926.

Gerlach, O.F.M. Cap., P. "Tijd en milieu van Jeroen Bosch." *Brabants Heem* 12 (1969) 110–118.

Göller, G., and H. Hilberath. *Musik in den Erkelenzer Landen*. Heinsberg: Kreis Heinsberg, 1972.

Gonnet, C. J., and R. D. Baart De La Faille. *Inventaris van het archief der stad Hoorn*. Haarlem, 1918.

Gotenberg, E. "Die Handschriften der Kölner Kreuzbrüder." Unpublished manuscript. Cologne, 1957.

Greb, F. L. "Zwei Gnadenbilder in der St. Lambertuskirche zu Düsseldorf." *Die Gottesmutter, Marienbild in Rheinland und Westfalen*. Ed. L. Küppers. Recklinghausen, 1974.

Grosche, A. *800 Jahre Stadt Medebach*. Medebach, 1951.

———. *Geschichte des Klosters Glindfeld*. Bigge, 1958.

Haass, R. "Devotio moderna in der Stadt Köln im 15. und 16. Jahrhundert." *Veröffentlichungen des Kölnischen Geschichtsvereins* 25 (1960) 134–154.

———. "Jakob Hoogen." *Clairlieu* 10 (1952) 54–62.

———. *Die Kreuzherren in den Rheinlanden*. Rheinisches Archiv. Veröffentlichungen des Instituts für Geschichtliche Landeskunde der Rheinlande an der Universität Bonn 23. Bonn, 1932.

———. "Prior Jakob Hoogen, ein führender Kopf der Aufklärung am Niederrhein." *Annalen des historischen Vereins für dem Niederrhein* 128 (1956) 210–225.

———. "Spätmittelalterliche Reformbestrebungen im niederrheinischen Raum und der Kreuzherrenorden." *Annalen des historischen Vereins für dem Niederrhein* 144–145 (1946–1947) 44–62.

Hannick, P. "Prieuré des Croisiers à Suxy." *Monasticon Belge* 5:339–344. Liege, 1975.

———. "Prieuré des Croisiers à Virton." *Monasticon Belge* 5:345–350. Liege, 1975.

Hayden, J. Michael. "The Crosiers in England and France." *Clairlieu* 22 (1964) 91–100.

_____. "The French Crosiers in the 17th and 18th Centuries." *Clairlieu* 27 (1969) 3-46.

Heere, O.S.C., L. "Bewoners, Weldoeners en vrienden van het Klooster te Maaseik in de jaren 1476-1797." *De Kruisheren te Maaseik.* Diest, 1955.

_____. "Dokumenten uit de statutenstrijd van 1765." *Clairlieu* 18 (1960) 71-80.

_____. "Een Hollands College ten Cruycenbroederen tot Colen." *Clairlieu* 7 (1949) 101-108.

_____. "Inventaris van het archief van het Kruisherenklooster te Maaseik." Unpublished manuscript.

_____. "De Kruisbroeders van Woudrichem." *Clairlieu* 8 (1950) 34-49.

_____. "De Kruisheren van Asperen." *Kruistriomf* (1956) 2-7, 37-41, 69-73.

_____. "De Kruisheren van Doornik." *Kruistriomf* (1951-1952) 2-6, 35-39, 67-70, 105-109, 173-178.

_____. "Het Kruisherenklooster te Maaseik voor de Franse Revolutie." *De Kruisheren te Maaseik.* Diest, 1955.

_____. "Het Kruisherenklooster te Venlo." *Publications de la soc. hist. et arch. dans le Limbourg* 92-93 (1956-1957) 235-368 and 94-95 (1958-1959) 209-300.

_____. "Een Maastrichtse Bibliofiel Prior Jan Proenen." *Clairlieu* 17 (1959) 3-17.

_____. "Matthijs Brouwers, Een excellente oeffinghe van het lijden ende passie O.H.J.C. ende wordt genaemt het cruysgebet." *Clairlieu* 18 (1960) 86-87.

_____. "Een Nederlands Antifoon." *Ons Geestlijk Erf* 26 (1952) 105-112.

_____. "Het Obituarium der Kruisheren van Roermond." *Publications de la soc. hist. et arch. dans le Limbourg* 90-91 (1954-1955) 51-125.

_____. "De oude gebruiken bij de Kruisheren." *Clairlieu* 3 (1945) 13-20.

_____. "Prieuré des Croisiers à Maaseik." *Monasticon Belge* 6:243-251. Liege, 1976.

_____. "Prieuré de Kolen à Kerniel." *Monasticon Belge* 6:253-259. Liege, 1976.

_____. "Het Roermondse Kruisherenklooster." *Publications de la soc. hist. et arch. dans le Limbourg* 76 (1941) 5-49.

_____. *600 Jaar Sint Agatha.* Cuijk: St. Agatha, 1971.

_____. "Het Sint-Petersdal of het Kruisbroederklooster te Hoorn." *Cruciferana* n.s. 22 (1964).

_____. "Studenten der Latijnse- en Hoogschool van Uden." *Clairlieu* 6 (1948) 53–65.

_____. "Uit de Librije van Sint-Petersdal de Hoorn." *Clairlieu* 9 (1951) 75–79.

_____. "Zielzorg in de kapel van de Grote Heilige Geest te Maastricht." *Maasgouw* 81 (1962) cols. 175–180.

Helbeck, G. "Hohlwege im Beyenberger Raum: Spuren einer alten König-, Pilger-, Heer- und Hansestrasse." *Kulturgeschichtliche Bodendenkmale im Raume Wuppertal.* Beiträge zur Geschichte und Heimatkunde des Wuppertals 24. N.p., 1976.

Helin, M. "Clairlieu au XVIᵉ siècle d'après le 'Journal de Roger de Nimègue.'" *Clairlieu* 9 (1951) 49–66.

Helyot, S. J. *Histoires des ordres monastiques, religieux et militaires.* Paris, 1714.

Hendriks, O. "Gerardus Geldenhouwer Noviomagus." *Studia Catholica* 31 (1956) 128–149, 176–196.

Hendriks, L. R. "Handschriften van Sint-Agatha." *Brabantia* 6 (1957) 249–265.

_____. "Johannes van Deventer, een bekend miniaturist uit Sint-Agatha." *Numaga* 5 (1958).

Hereswitha (Sister). "Orde van het Heilig-Graf." *Inleidung tot de geschiedenis van het kloosterwezen in de Nederlanden.* A: Orden onstaan in de Middeleeuwen. Brussels, 1975.

Hermann, W. *Zur Geschichte der Neisser Kreuzherren vom Orden der regulierten Chorherren und Wächter des Heiligen Grabes zu Jerusalem mit dem doppelten roten Kreuz.* Breslau, 1938.

Hermans, C. R. *Annales Canonicorum Regularium S. Augustini Ordinis Sanctae Crucis.* 3 vols. 's Hertoogenbosch, 1858. *Index.* Diest, 1953.

Hertzworms, O.S.C., A. *Religio sanctissimae Crucis.* Roermond, 1686.

Het Land van Cuijk, kerkelijk en politiek verleden. Cuijk, 1971. (Collected papers of a historical congress held at Cuijk in 1971.)

Hofmeister, Ph. "Die Verfassung des holländischen Kreuzherrenordens." *Festschrift Ulrich Stutz.* (= *Kirchenrechtliche Abhandlungen* 117–118.) Stuttgart, 1938.

Honhon, O.S.C., L. *De heilige Odilia, maagd en martelares, Patrones van de orde der Kruisheren.* Roermond, 1887.

———. *De stichting der Kruisherenmissie in den Congo-Uele.* Diest, 1922.

———. *Theodorus de Celles. Eerste Generaal en stichter der Orde van het H. Kruis.* Diest, 1936.

Hörmann, M. *Die augustiner Chorherren in Augsburg im Mittelalter.* Bottrop, 1932.

Hostie, R. *Leven en dood van de religieuse instituten.* Eammaus, 1972.

Huenecke, W. *Das Kloster Lilienthal und die Gemeinde Falkenhagen.* Detmold, 1897.

Husman, J., and Th. Trippel. *Geschichte der ehemaligen Herrlichkeit bzw. Reichsgrafschaft und der Pfarre Wickrath.* Giesenkirchen, 1911.

Huybers, O.S.C., Th. "Een philosophische cursus van Kruisheer L. de Fisen, 1728-1729." *Clairlieu* 10 (1952) 3-26.

Huygens, C. *Lettres de Jacques de Vitry.* Leiden, 1960.

Hymnarium Sanctae Agathae, bevattende de sequenties uit het Graduale van Johannes van Deventer. Cuijk: St. Agatha, 1955.

Inhoud en waarde van regel en constituties der Kruisheren. Diest, 1957. (Collected papers from a seminar held at the Crosier monastery in Maaseik, Belgium, in 1957.)

Jamar, J. T. J. *Inventaris van het archief van het klooster der Kruisheren te Roermond.* Maastricht, 1973.

Janssen, R. "De Maaseiker Historiografie." *Maaslandse Sprokkelingen* n.s. 4 (1978).

Joris, A. *Le visage de Huy.* Brussels, 1976.

Jung, W. *Oppenheim und seine Katherinenkirche.* Königstein-im-Taunus, n.d.

Kami Yang Ditandi Salib Suci. Bandung, 1977.

Kirschbaum, J. *Liturgische Handschriften aus dem Kölner Fraterhaus St. Michael am Weidenbach und ihre Stellung in der Kölner Buchmalerei des 16. Jahrhunderts.* Bonn, 1972.

———. "Eine Kölner Handschrift des frühen 14. Jahrhunderts." *Beiträge zur rheinischen Kunstgeschichte und Denkmalpflege* 2. Düsseldorf, 1974.

Kisky, W., and R. Knipping. *Die Regesten der Erzbischöfe von Köln im Mittelalter.* Bonn, 1901-1915.

Kittel, E. "Das Kreuzherrenkloster Falkenhagen." *Dona Westfalica Georg Schrüber zum 80. Geburtstag.* Münster, 1963.

Klompen, W. *Die Säkularisation im Arrondissement Krefeld.* Kempen, 1962.

Knipping, R. *Niederrheinische Archivalien in der Nationalbibliothek und dem Nationalarchiv zu Paris.* Leipzig, 1904.

Knowles, D. *The Religious Orders in England.* Cambridge, 1962.

Lacomblet, Th. J. *Urkundenbuch für die Geschichte des Niederrhein.* 4 vols. Düsseldorf, 1840–1857.

Lantin, O.S.C., A. *Gedenkboek voor vierentwintig bloedgetuigen van de Kruisheren-orde in de missielanden Kongo en Irian Barat.* Diest, 1966.

Le Blanc, O.S.C., Th. C. *Symbolum Trinitatis.* Roermond, 1668.

Lectures on Crosier Spirituality. Trans. F. Jutte, O.S.C. and others. Fort Wayne, Ind., 1957. (English translation of papers delivered at a seminar on Crosier spirituality held at the Crosier monastery in Maaseik, Belgium, in 1954.)

Les manuscrits des Croisiers de Huy, Liège et Cuijk. Exposition catalogue. Liege, 1951.

Lichter, E. "Strassenbau am Ausgang des Kurstaates Trier." *Neues Trierisches Jahrbuch* (special edition, 1964).

———. *Welschbillig und Umgebung.* Trier, 1977.

———. "200 Jahre neue Wallfahrtskirche Helenenberg bei Welschbillig." *Neues Trierisches Jahrbuch* (1966) 90–101.

Lorenz, W. *Die Kreuzherren mit dem roten Stern.* Königstein, 1964.

Marcus, A. F. *Klooster Marienlof Kolen-Kerniel.* Beeringen, 1972.

Melart, L. *Histoire de la ville et chasteau de Huy et ses antiquitez, avec une chronologie des ses comtes et évesques.* Tournai, 1641.

Menne, K. *Deutsche und Niederlandische Handschriften.* 4 vols. Cologne, 1941.

Mens, O.F.M. Cap., A. "De 'Kleine Armen van Christus' in de Brabantse-Luikse gewesten." *Ons Geestlijk Erf* 36 (1962) 282–331, 37 (1963) 129–169 and 353–401, 38 (1964) 113–144, 39 (1965) 225–271.

———. *Oorsprong en betekenis van de Nederlandse Begijnen- en Bogardenbeweging.* Antwerp, 1949.

Meijer, G. A. "Een Ordinarium der Kruisheren." *Archief voor de Geschiedenis van het Aartsbisdom Utrecht* 41 (1915) 97–194.

Mischke, O.S.C., B. *Odilia, Maid of the Cross.* Onamia, Minn.: Crosier Press, 1955.

Moreau, S.J., E. "L'origines des Croisiers Belges." *Clairlieu* 3 (1945) 7-12.

Noordeloos, P. "Een bijdrage tot de geschiedenis van de Commanderie van St. Antonius van Maastricht." *Publications de la soc. hist. et arch. dans le Limbourg* 92-93 (1956-1957) 153-254.

Padberg, C. F. *Küstelberg, Geschichte eines hochsauerländischen Dorfes.* Medebach-Küstelberg, 1975.

Persoons, E. "Handschriften uit kloosters in de Nederlanden te Wenen." *Archief- en Bibliotheekwezen in België* 38 (1967) 59-107.

Piccardt, R. A. S. *Bijzonderheden uit de geschiedenis der stad Goes.* Goes, 1865.

Plag, O.S.C., H. " 'Iter Para tutum.' Bij het vijfde lustrum van de Kruisheren in Brazilië." *Chronicon Cruciferorum* 2, fasc. 3, 221-254.

Post, R. R. "De oorsprong van de orde der Kruisbroeders." *Archief voor de geschiedenis van de katholieke kerk in Nederland* (1963) 243-253.

Raedschelders, O.S.C., L., ed. *Buta 1965.* Opglabbeek: Paesen, 1990.

Ramaekers, O.S.C., A. "The Crosier Order as a Canonical Order." *Lectures on Crosier Spirituality.* Fort Wayne, Ind., 1957.

_____. "De Kruisherenaflaat." *Clairlieu* 6 (1948) 3-52.

_____. "Oudheidkundige, Dr. H. van Lieshout." *Het Oude Land van Loon* 1 (1945) 1-7.

_____. "De privileges der Kruisherenorde vanaf haar onstaan tot aan het concilie van Trente." *Clairlieu* 1 (1943) 9-83.

Rausch, O.S.C., J. *The Crosier Story: A History of the Crosier Fathers in the United States.* Onamia, Minn.: Crosier Press, 1960.

Redlich, O. *Kirchenpolitik in Jülich-Berg am Ausgang des Mittelalters und in der Reformationzeit.* 2 vols. Bonn, 1907-1915.

Reicke, S. *Das Deutsche Spital und sein Recht im Mittelalter.* 2 vols. Stuttgart, 1942.

Reiners, H. *Die Kunstdenkmäler van Eupen-Malmedy.* Düsseldorf, n.d.

Reussens, E. "Documents relatifs à l'histoire de l'Université de Louvain, 1425-1797." *Analectes pour servir à l'histoire ecclésiastique de la Belgique* 23 (1892) 212-219.

Richstätter, K. *Altdeutsche heilige Stunde zu Ehren des heiligsten Herzens Jesu.* Munich, 1938.

Roger, P. *Notices historiques sur Virton.* Virton, 1932.

Röhricht, R. "Briefe des Jacobus de Vitriaco." *Zeitschrift für Kirchengeschichte* 15 (1894) 97–120.

Römer, F. C. M. "De kloosters in Goes." *Zeeuwse Volksalmanak* (1845) 6–19.

Roppe, L., A. Dusar, and M. Colson, O.S.C. *Het Odiliaschrijn, Klooster Kolen-Kerniel.* Hasselt, 1965.

Röttgen, B. *Brüggen und Born im Schwalmtal.* Kempen, 1934.

Russelius, O.S.C., H. *Chronicon Cruciferorum sive Synopsis Memorabilium Sacri et Canonici Ordinis Sanctae Crucis.* Cologne: H. Kraft, 1635. Photographic reproduction, Diest, 1964.

Sandburg, J. F. "Archivalia van het klooster der Kruisbroeders te Schiedam 1443–1554." Unpublished and undated manuscript belonging to the Algem. Rijksarchief of 's Gravenhage.

Sangers, O.S.C., W. *Father Eduard Daems, O.S.C., 1826–1879, de vader van de kolonisten in Wisconsin.* Xaveriana 187. Louvain, 1939.

_____. "De oudste constituties der Kruisherenorde." *Miscellanea L. van der Essen.* Brussels, 1947.

_____. "Predikbroeders-Kruisbroeders." *Miscellanea Gessleriana.* Antwerp, 1948.

_____, and G. Van Der Linden. *De Kruisheren te Diest 1845–1945.* Diest, 1945.

Sauerland, H. V. *Urkunden und Regesten zur Geschichte der Rheinlande aus dem vatikanischen Archiv.* 7 vols. Bonn, 1902–1913.

Scheerder, O.S.C., J. "Henricus Martinus Franciscus Hollmann, 52ste Magister Generaal de Orde van het H. Kruis, 1853–1927." *Clairlieu* 23–24 (1965–1966).

_____. *Henricus van den Wijmelenberg; een religieuse emancipator in Oost-Brabant 1800–1881. De nieuwe lente in de orde van het H. Kruis.* Bijdragen tot de geschiedenis van het zuiden van Nederland 35. Tilburg, 1976.

_____. "Kruisheer L. G. J. Honhon, 1858–1942." *Clairlieu* 35 (1977) 3–88.

_____. "De Kruisheren van Sint-Agatha en Uden in de jaren 1800–1840." *Clairlieu* 31 (1973) 3–54.

_____. "De onderhandelingen over de terugkeer van de Kruisheren te Venlo." *Clairlieu* 34 (1976) 11–64.

_____. *Prior A. G. van Mil.* Diest, 1967.

Schellekens, O.S.C., R. "Rotterdam, Herinneringen aan de stichting van klooster en parochie." *Chronicon Cruciferorum* 1, fasc. 3:231-256.

Schoolmeesters, E. "Les regesta de Raoul de Zaehringen, Prince-évêque de Liège, 1167-1191." *Bulletin de la soc. d'art et d'histoire du diocèse de Liège* 1 (1881) 129-203.

Schuitema Meyer, A. F. *Het klooster Ter Apel.* Groningen, 1966.

Snijders, O.S.C., D. *Herman Linnebank 1875-1927. Zijn werk als criticus en Vlamingenvriend.* Antwerp, 1952.

Swoboda, Ph. I. *Gloriosa crucis memoria in expositione historica de ortu et progressu sacri ac antiquissimi canonici ordinis Crucigerorum cum rubeo corde, sancta Maria Demetrii de urbe, beatorum Martyrum de poenitentia sub regula divi Augustini militantes.* Prague, 1748.

Telting, A. "Het Kruisbroedersklooster te Franeker." *Vrije Vries* 9 (1862) 104-112.

Terboven, J. H. "Hohenbusch, ein ehemalige Kreuzherrenkloster." *Heimatkalendar Geilenkirchen-Heinsberg* (1965) 101-106.

Theele, J. "Aus der Bibliothek des Kölner Kreuzherrenklosters." *Mittelalterliche Handschriften. Festschrift für M. Degering.* Cologne, 1926.

Thomas, O.P., A. *De oudste constituties van de Dominicanen.* Louvain, 1965.

Van Apeldoorn, L. J. *De Kerkelijke goederen in Friesland.* 2 vols. Leeuwarden, 1915.

Van Asseldonk, O.S.C., A. "Aegidius de Vriese, dichter en leraar aan de Latijnse school te Maaseik." *De Kruisheren te Maaseik.* Diest, 1955.

_____. "Het Brevier van de Kruisheren." *Clairlieu* 3 (1944) 8-144.

_____. "Franciscus Vaes van Tongeren." *Clairlieu* 15-16 (1957-1958).

_____. "Handschriften van Kruisheren." *Clairlieu* 14 (1956) 65-87.

_____. "Handschriften van Kruisheren uit de XVe en XVIe eeuw over het ontstaan der orde van het H. Kruis." *Clairlieu* 3 (1944) 32-45.

_____. "Keulse Kruisherenhandschriften te Wenen." *Clairlieu* 27 (1969) 47-64.

_____. "Marginalia bij 'De pastoors van Heppeneert.'" *Clairlieu* 8 (1950) 67-80.

_____. "Middelleeuwse gebeden in Udens 16e eeuwse Brevier."
Clairlieu 12 (1954) 17-38.

_____. "De Odilia-preek van 1439 te Hoei." *Clairlieu* 17 (1959)
26-52.

_____. "De ouders van Franciscus Daems." *Clairlieu* 11 (1953)
42-44.

Van Dal, O.S.C., C. "Cistercienzer Literatuur op Kruisherenlibrar-
ia." *Cîteaux in de Nederlanden* 7 (1956) 291-294.

_____. "Rond Vestis nuptialis." *Clairlieu* 11 (1953) 3-29.

_____. "Sint Bernardus invloed op Pierre Pinchar, O.S.C." *Cîteaux
in de Nederlanden* 8 (1957) 165-180.

_____. *Volg mij. De Kruisheren in de Geschiedenis.* Diest, 1956.

Vandenberghe, R. *Damme.* Damme, n.d.

Van Den Bosch, O.S.C., J. "De H. Kruis- en Passiecultus in het
geestlijk leven der Kruisbroeders." *Cruciferana* n.s. 7 (1942).

_____. "Le couvent des Croisiers de Lannoy, 1474-1792." *Clairlieu*
13 (1955) 3-43.

Van Den Bosch, O.S.C., P. "De bibliotheken van de Kruisherenkloosters in de Nederlanden vóór 1550." *Studies over het boekenbezit en boekengebruik in de Nederlanden vóór 1660.* Brussels,
1974.

_____. "Brandenburg." *Clairlieu* 35 (1977) 93-95.

_____. "Chauny." *Clairlieu* 30 (1972) 84-86.

_____. "Düsseldorf. Ein Rückblick auf eine Ausstellung." *Clairlieu*
35 (1977) 95-106.

_____. "De 'Enquête' van Prof. J. le Goff." *Clairlieu* 31 (1973)
123-125.

_____. *Das Kloster Lilienthal zu Falkenhagen.* Falkenhagen, 1978.

_____. "De orde van de Kruisheren in het verleden een hospitaalor-
de?" *Handelingen van het XLIe congres van de Federatie van de
Kringen voor Oudheidkeit en Geschiedenis van België.* Mechelen,
1970.

_____. "De Priorij Sint Helena te Scharmer, 1489-1596." *Clairlieu*
33 (1975) 3-30.

_____. "Schwarzenbroich. Noch einmal über die Familie von Mer-
ode." *Clairlieu* 35 (1977) 114-125.

_____. "Studien over de observantie der Kruisbroeders in de vijf-
tiende eeuw." *Clairlieu* 26 (1968) 3-205.

_____. "Thomas van Kempen en de Kruisheren." *Archief voor de
geschiedenis van de katholieke Kerk in Nederland* 13 (1971)
277-307.

_____. "De 500. Verjaring van de boekdrukkunst." *Clairlieu* 34 (1976) 104-108.

_____. "Winterberg." *Clairlieu* 32 (1974) 77-80.

Van De Pasch, O.S.C., A. "Een commentaar op de statuten." *Clairlieu* 7 (1949) 40-53.

_____. *De definities der generale kapittels van de orde van het H. Kruis, 1410-1786.* Brussels, 1969.

_____. "De drie Gradualia." *Clairlieu* 7 (1949) 65-100.

_____. "Kapittelbesluiten van het Kruisherenklooster te Keulen 1679-1789." *Clairlieu* 33 (1975) 31-58.

_____. "Het klooster Clairlieu te Hoei en zijn prioren-generaal." *Clairlieu* 17 (1959) 65-112 and 18 (1960) 13-70.

_____. "Het Kruisherenklooster van Glindfeld 1499-1804." *Clairlieu* 10 (1952) 41-53.

_____. "Monastère des Croisiers à Huy." *Monasticon Belge* 2:405-413. Liege, 1962.

_____. "Monastère des Croisiers à Liège." *Monasticon Belge* 2:415-422. Liege, 1962.

_____. "Prior Henricus Walteri Verheyen 1584-1647." *Clairlieu* 32 (1974) 3-74.

_____. "De Tekst van de constituties der Kruisheren van 1248." *Hand. Kon. Comm. Gesch. Brussel* 117 (1952) 1-96.

_____. "Uit een Devotieboekje van de vroegere Klaaskerk te Venlo." *Clairlieu* 34 (1976) 3-10.

Van De Ven, A. J. "Het Kruisbroedersconvent te Schiedam." *Bijdragen voor de geschiedenis van het bisdom Haarlem* 43 (1925) 368-422.

Van De Ven, O.S.C., H. "Kruisheren." *Theologische Woordenboek* cols. 2819-2828. Roermond-Maaseik, 1957.

Van De Ven, T. J. "Dr. C. R. Hermans, Leven en werk van de pionier van de Noordbrabantse geschiedschrijving in de 19e eeuw." *Brabantia* 7 (1958) 183-206, 211-234.

Van Hasselt, O.S.C., H. P. A. "Geschiedenis van het klooster der Kruisheren te Maastricht." *Publications de la soc. hist. et arch. dans le Limbourg* 39 (1903) 1-137.

_____. "Geschiedenis van het klooster der Kruisheren te Wickrath." *Geschiedk. Bladen* 2 (1906) 17-37.

Van Lieshout, O.S.C., H. *Rond het reliekschrijn van Sint Odilia.* Hasselt, 1935.

Van Luijk, B. "Het Kruisherenideaal en de intensivering van de volkszielzorg in de 13e eeuw." *Het Oude Land van Loon* 16 (1961) 135-147.

Van Rooijen, O.S.C., H. "The Church of the Holy Cross *de Claro Loco* and the True Origins of the Crosiers: A Spiritual Drama." Trans. M. Cotone, O.S.C. Unpublished manuscript.

_____. "A History of the Crosier Order. An Endeavour." Mimeographed text of a course on Crosier history delivered at the United States Crosier major seminary in Fort Wayne, Indiana, during the 1961-1962 school year.

_____. "Het klooster in het polderland." *In Cruce Vita. De orde der Kruisheren in Nederland.* Rotterdam, 1936.

_____. "Kruisheren." *Liturgisch Woordenboek* 2, cols. 1397-1405. Roermond-Maaseik, 1958-1967.

_____. "The Liturgy of the Crosiers." *Crosier Heritage* 10 (September, 1983) 1-6.

_____. *De oorsprong van de orde der Kruisbroeders of Kruisheren. De Geschiedbronnen.* Diest, 1961.

_____. *Sinte Odilia, legende of historie?* Diest, 1945.

_____. *Theodorus van Celles. Een tijds- en levensbeeld.* Cuijk: St. Agatha, 1936.

Van Schilfgaarde, R. A. P. *Het archief der Heeren en Graven van Culemborg.* 's Gravenhage, 1949.

Vennenbusch, J. *Die theologischen Handschriften des Stadtarchivs Köln.* Teil I: Die Folio-Handschriften der Gymnasiabibliothek (Mitteilungen aus dem Stadtarchiv von Köln). Cologne and Vienna, 1976.

Verduc, O.S.C., P. *La vie du bienheureux Théodore de Celles.* Perigeux, 1681.

Verhoeven, O.S.C., J. *Gijzelaars onder Makondo.* Diest, 1965.

Vinken, O.S.C., M. "Croisiers." *Dictionnaire d'histoire et de géographie ecclésiastiques* 13, cols. 1042-1062. N.p., n.d.

_____. "Crosiers." *Dictionnaire de spiritualité,* cols. 2573-2575. N.p., n.d.

_____. "Le culte marial chez les Croisiers." *Maria, études sur la sainte Vierge.* Paris, 1949.

_____. *The Spirituality of the Crosier Fathers.* Trans. B. Van Gils, O.S.C. Syracuse, Ind., 1957.

Von Roden, G. *Geschichte der Stadt Duisburg.* Bd. I: Das alte Duisburg von den Anfängen bis 1905. Duisburg, 1970.

Von Steynitz, J. *Mittelalterliche Hospitäler der Orden und Städte als Einrichtungen der sozialen Sicherung.* Sozialpolitische Schriften 26. Berlin, 1970.

Von Witzleben, E. "Kölner Bibelfenster des 15. Jahrhunderts in Schottland, England und Amerika," *Aachener Kunstblätter* 43 (1972) 227-248.

Wamper, H. *Das Leben der Brüder Adrian und Peter van Walenburch aus Rotterdam und ihr Wirken in der Erzdiözese Köln bis zum Jahre 1649.* Cologne, 1968.

Weisbein, N. "Le 'laudes crucis attolamus' de maître Hugues d'Orleans, dit le primas." *Revue du moyen âge latin* 3 (1947) 5-26.

Weiss, H. U. *Die Kreuzherren in Westfalen.* Diest, 1963.

Wester, O.S.C., G. "In de Gordel van Smaragd." *In Cruce Vita. De orde der Kruisheren in Nederland.* Rotterdam, 1936.

————. "In Rotterdam's groene gordel." *In Cruce Vita. De orde der Kruisheren in Nederland.* Rotterdam, 1936.

Wetzel, W. "Paläographische Beobachtungen an datierten Handschriften des Kölner Kreuzbrüderskloster." Unpublished manuscript. Cologne, 1968.

Wilmotte, L. *Notice historique sur le couvent des Croisiers de Huy.* Huy, n.d.

Zimmermann, W. "Jakob Hoogen (1742-1805), Prior des Kreuzherrenklosters und Pfarrer in Wegberg, der führende Aufklärer und Pädagoge am Neiderrhein." *Rhein. Vierteljahrsbl.* 19 (1954) 227-248.

————. "Ein Nachwort zu 'Jakob Hoogen' (1742-1805)." *Rhein. Vierteljahrsbl.* 19 (1954) 248-249.